1417

1260
(8)

This book is to be returned on or before
the last date stamped below.

D1341238

A Methuen Paperback

First published in 1986
as a paperback original
by Methuen London Ltd,
11 New Fetter Lane, London EC4P 4EE
and Methuen Inc, 29 West 35th Street,
New York, NY 10001

Copyright in the compilation
© 1986 by Nick Worrall
Copyright in the series format
© 1986 by Methuen London Ltd
Copyright in editorial presentation
© 1986 by Simon Trussler

Typeset in IBM 9pt Press Roman
by 🅣 Tek-Art, Croydon, Surrey
Printed in Great Britain by
Richard Clay (The Chaucer Press) Ltd,
Bungay, Suffolk

British Library Cataloguing Publication Data

File on Chekov (Writer-Files)
    1. Chekhov, A.P. – Criticism and interpretaion
    I. Title   II. Series
    891.72'3   PG3458

    ISBN 0–413–53740–4 Pbk

*Cover image based on a photo
from the Mansell Collection*

Contents

The theatre is, by its nature, an ephemeral art: yet it is a daunting task to track down the newspaper reviews, or contemporary statements from the writer or his director, which are often all that remain to help us recreate some sense of what a particular production was like. This series is therefore intended to make readily available a selection of the comments that the critics made about the plays of leading modern dramatists at the time of their production — and to trace, too, the course of each writer's own views about his work and his world.

In addition to combining a uniquely convenient source of such elusive *documentation*, the 'Writer-Files' series also assembles the *information* necessary for readers to pursue further their interest in a particular writer or work. Variations in quantity between one writer's output and another, differences in temperament which make some readier than others to talk about their work, and the variety of critical response, all mean that the presentation and balance of material shifts between one volume and another: but we have tried to arrive at a format for the series which will nevertheless enable users of one volume readily to find their way around any other.

Section 1, 'A Brief Chronology', provides a quick conspective overview of each playwright's life and career. *Section 2* deals with the plays themselves, arranged chronologically in the order of their composition: information on first performances, major revivals, and publication is followed by a brief synopsis (for quick reference set in slightly larger, italic type), then by a representative selection of the critical response, and of the dramatist's own comments on the play and its theme.

Section 3 offers concise guidance to each writer's work in non-dramatic forms, while *Section 4* provides a bibliographical guide to other primary and secondary sources of further reading, among which full details will be found of works cited elsewhere under short titles, and of collected editions of the plays — but not of individual titles, particulars of which will be found with the other factual data in Section 2.

The 'Writer-Files' series hopes by striking this kind of balance between information and a wide range of opinion to offer 'companions' to a study of major playwrights in the modern repertoire — not in that dangerous pre-digested fashion which can too readily

General Editor's Introduction

5

quench the desire to read the plays themselves, nor so prescriptively as to allow any single line of approach to predominate, but rather to encourage readers to form their own judgements of the plays, to set against the many views here represented.

The beginning student of Chekhov, perhaps knowing the major plays but little else, will quickly become aware through this volume of the huge quantity and variety of the other work he produced, notably in the form of the short story. Interestingly, too, one begins to realize how Chekhov found his way into theatre through such exploratory forms as the short monologue, vaudeville sketch, and anecdotal one-acter, as if an already-mature writer were flexing unaccustomed muscles in a new medium.

The compiler here has tackled the problem of introducing the enormous body of Chekhov's non-dramatic prose through an evocative survey of its changing preoccupations and moods. We are thus granted a fuller context than was enjoyed by most of Chekhov's early critics, and this casts its own light on the seeming obsession of so many of them with whether Chekhov's great plays were classically tragic, evoked a peculiarly Russian melancholy which was difficult to imitate further west, or were essentially the comedies Chekhov himself so often proclaimed them − as in a number of the letters to his early directors and actors here reproduced.

The problem is made more complex by the fact that the virtual father of modern acting style, Stanislavsky, made his own reputation with the Moscow Art Theatre productions of the later plays, which have therefore tended to become identified with the naturalistic style for which Stanislavsky gave actors their ways and means. In truth, Chekhov was his own, not Stanislavsky's man, and in consequence many of the critics here represented are as illuminating for the light they shed on theatrical and critical fashions as on the plays themselves. Thankfully, the sheer range of comment here included makes it necessary for each reader to arrive at his or her own conclusions − in the consciousness that, like all great plays, Chekhov's will continue both to absorb and transcend the changing moods of passing times.

Simon Trussler

1860   17 Jan., born in Taganrog, a port in Southern Russia, son of a grocer, third of six children. His paternal grandfather was a peasant who bought his freedom in 1841, twenty years before the emancipation of the serfs. Tyrannical and religious upbringing (according to brother Alexander: more sympathetic versions offered by brother Michael and sister Masha).

1867   Aged seven, enrolled, together with elder brother Nicholas, at school attached to local Greek Orthodox Church.

1868   Entered Taganrog grammar school (until 1879). An average pupil. Acquired a reputation as practical joker and storyteller. Attacks of peritonitis: not a healthy child.

1876   Father in financial difficulties. Family left Taganrog for Moscow, leaving Chekhov behind to continue schooling. Supported himself by coaching.

1877   First visit to Moscow. Enjoyed the theatre, and *Uncle Tom's Cabin*, Mayne Reid, Buckle, Victor Hugo, Schopenhauer, and von Humboldt; also Russian radical thinkers and literary critics, Belinsky, Dobrolyubov, Pisarev. Wrote a stage farce, *Diamond Cut Diamond* (or *Scythe Strikes Stone*).

1878   Wrote full-length serious play *Fatherless* and vaudeville *Not for Nothing Did the Chicken Sing* (*Why the Hen Clucks*), both now lost.

1879   Placed eleventh out of 23 in final exams. 8 Aug., moved to Moscow to join family living in a basement flat in a brothel district. Enrolled in the Medical Faculty of Moscow University for a five-year period. Practical experience gained in summer vacations at local hospital.

1880   9 Mar., two stories published in humorous magazine *The Dragonfly*, a Petersburg weekly. Ten pseudonymous contributions in all.

1881   Abandoned *The Dragonfly* for Moscow publications *The Alarm Clock* and *The Spectator*. Two articles on visiting actress Sarah Bernhardt.

1882   Four times as much material published than previous year. Debut in Petersburg weekly *Fragments*. Ninety-page parody of Hungarian novelist serialized in

The Alarm Clock. A Nasty Story published about an artist who proposes by asking the girl to become his model, and *Belated Blossom* which foreshadows *The Cherry Orchard*. A full-length play, probably *Platonov*, submitted to Yermolova at the Moscow Maly Theatre and rejected.

1883 Ninety pieces published in Petersburg weekly *Oskolki*, for whom he began a regular column *Fragments of Moscow Life*. First published book, *Fairy Tales of Melpomene*.

1884 Total humorous stories in various magazines had risen to 300 by end of year. *The Shooting Party*, a mystery thriller and his only novel-length work, published in 32 instalments in *Daily News*. June, graduated from university as qualified doctor. Took up temporary duties at Chikino rural hospital. Dec., first signs of the tuberculosis which was to kill him.

1885 More than 100 short stories, some more serious in tone. 29 May, one-act *On the High Road* rejected by the censor. First stories under his own name submitted to *New Times*, Petersburg publication owned by Alexey Suvorin.

1886 15 Feb., first contribution to *New Times*. Previous six years had seen 372 titles under various pseudonyms, two-thirds of which Chekhov excluded from his *Collected Works*. Interest in Darwin and developing interest in music. *Motley Tales* published, mid-May. Moved with family to a two-storey house, and became briefly engaged to 'a Jewish lady', probably Dunya Efros, a friend of the family. One-acter *On the Harmfulness of Tobacco*.

1887 Third book of selected stories published, *In the Twilight*. Jan., first published vaudeville, *Swan Song*, written 'in an hour and five minutes'. A 'comedy', *Ivanov*, commissioned by Moscow theatre proprietor, Korsh, and performed at the Korsh Theatre, 19 Nov. Furore.

1888 19 Feb., premiere of *Swan Song* at Korsh Theatre. Mar., long short story *The Steppe* published in Petersburg monthly, *The Northern Herald*, his first appearance in a serious literary review. One-act vaudeville *The Bear* written in Feb. and staged in Oct. Began work on full-length play *The Wood Demon*, under influence of Tolstoy. Wrote one-act vaudeville *The Proposal*. Oct., awarded the Pushkin Prize 'for the best literary production distinguished by high artistic merit'. Met Stanislavsky and Tchaikovsky. Dec., revised *Ivanov* for the first Petersburg production at the Aleksandrinsky Theatre while supervising production of Suvorin's play *Tatyana Repina* at the Korsh.

1889   17 Jan., death of his brother Nicholas from tuberculosis. 31 Jan., premiere of *Ivanov*: great success. Collection of stories *Children* published, also short story *The Princess* and novella *A Dreary Story*. Completed one-act plays *The Wedding* and *A Tragedian despite Himself*. May, draft of *The Wood Demon* completed. Rejected by the Aleksandrinsky and Maly, but sold to Abramova Theatre in Moscow, and opened 27 Dec., to hostile notices for only three performances.

1890   Mar., volume of stories *Gloomy People* published. 21 Apr., set out on journey by horse, rail, and steamer, arriving July, to the convict settlement on Sakhalin island, off Russia's eastern seaboard: motives scientific, humanitarian, and literary. Conducted census of about 10,000 convicts, averaging 160 interviews a day. Notes written up as nine travel articles for *New Times*, published betwen July and Aug. 13 Oct., left Sakhalin, travelling via Hong Kong, Singapore, Ceylon ('very beautiful'), and Suez Canal, arriving Odessa 1 Dec. Resumed life in Moscow with family in new premises.

1891   Began work on non-fictional study *The Island of Sakhalin*. Story *The Duel* serialized in *New Times*. Six-week tour of western Europe in company with Suvorin. 19 Mar., Vienna. 22 Mar., Venice, 'a most wonderful city'. Bologna, Florence, and Rome spoiled by cultural satiety and bad weather. Liked Naples and Pompeii. Impressed by Vesuvius. Nice, Monte Carlo, Paris. Back in Russia, rented dacha at Bogimovo. Intensification of his relationship with Lika Mizinova, a friend of his sister's. Sept., worked on *An Anonymous Story* and his last completed one-act vaudeville, *The Anniversary (The Jubilee)*. Started a subscription to aid famine victims. Wrote *The Grasshopper*. Severe influenza with lung complications.

1892   Jan., famine relief mission to Nizhny Novgorod province. Feb., relief expedition to Voronezh. Mar., purchased estate of Melikhovo, 50 miles from Moscow. Continued to practice medicine, build schools, plant fruit trees, cultivate fir, pine, larch, and oak trees, grow flowers, stock fishponds, and run the estate as a self-supporting commune growing its own cereal and vegetables. His medical 'diocese' covered 26 villages and seven factories. One of his best-known stories, *Ward 6*, published in Nov.

1894   Excursion to Crimea in Mar., and further expedition to western Europe, Sept. Trieste, Milan, Genoa, Paris, Berlin. Twelve new stories published, including *Three Years* and *Ariadne*.

9

1895 *The Seagull* written, Oct.-Nov. Met Tolstoy at Yasnaya Polyana: increasingly critical of his teachings.

1896 *My Life* published in monthly instalments in *Niva*. 17 Oct., premiere of *The Seagull* at Alexandrinsky Theatre. Komissarzhevskaya as Nina, a benefit performance. A disaster; but subsequent performances more favourably received. Dec., first reference in a letter to *Uncle Vanya*.

1897 Story *Peasants* published in Apr. *Collected Plays* published, including *Uncle Vanya*. Some provincial performances of *Vanya* recorded between now and 1899. 22 Mar., experienced a violent lung haemorrage, and a further attack led to his removal to a clinic from where he was discharged on 10 Apr. Tuberculosis diagnosed. Sept., convalesence for eight months in Nice. Resumed creative writing in Oct. Became interested in the Dreyfus case and sided with Zola in championing the French Officer's innocence. Cooled towards Suvorin and the anti-semitic line taken by the reactionary *New Times*.

1898 Health appeared to have improved. 2 May, returned to Melikhovo. Wrote *A Hard Case, Gooseberries,* and *Concerning Love* during the summer. Approached by Nemirovich-Danchenko with request for new Moscow Art Theatre to stage *The Seagull* during their first season. Sept., decided to move to Yalta to avoid Moscow winter but spent a few days in Moscow. Attended rehearsals of *The Seagull*, and also of *Tsar Fyodor Ioannovich*, where he was attracted to the actress Olga Knipper. 18 Sept., arrived in Yalta, where he stayed for seven months. Commissioned the building of a villa on a plot bought for 4000 roubles and also bought a cottage eighteen miles further along the coast. 12 Oct., death of his father. Nov.-Dec., wrote four new stories, including *The Darling*. Nov., first communication with Maxim Gorky. 17 Dec., premiere of *The Seagull* at the Moscow Art Theatre: tremendous success.

1899 Sold copyright of his works for 75,000 roubles to Petersburg publisher, A.F. Marks, but reserved performance rights, which were bringing in royalties of 1,000 roubles a year. Formidable task undertaken to assemble and read his entire published work: *Collected Works* appeared in ten volumes between 1899 and 1902. 19 Mar., first meeting with Gorky in Yalta. Organized subscription for sanatorium for consumption sufferers. Apr., travelled to Moscow, where he became entangled in controversy over *Uncle Vanya* with Maly Theatre, and eventually handed the play to the Moscow Art Theatre. 1 May, special performance of

The Seagull attended by Chekhov, who disapproved of the interpretation. 16 June, first letter to Knipper (their correspondence
eventually ran to three volumes of 1,000 items). Aug., Melikhovo
sold. Knipper visited Chekhov in Yalta and returned with him to
Moscow. Spent next eight months in Yalta, in new villa nearing
completion. 26 Oct., premiere of *Uncle Vanya:* a qualified success.
Oct.-Dec., wrote *The Lady with the Little Dog* and *In the Ravine*,
more or less last short stories. First thoughts of *Three Sisters.*

1900 Worked on *Three Sisters* most of the year. Jan., elected
to the Academy of Sciences. Slight improvement in health. Two-
week Crimean tour by Moscow Art Theatre beginning Sevastopol,
10 Apr. Company spent ten days with Chekhov in Yalta. May,
toured the Caucasus with Gorky and the painter Vasnetsov. First
draft of *Three Sisters* completed in Oct., and read to the
company in Nov. Dec., to Nice. Relationship with Knipper
deepened.

1901 31 Jan., premiere of *Three Sisters* with Knipper as Masha.
Jan., third tour of Italy. 25 May, marriage to Knipper in Moscow,
and honeymoon in S.E. Russia, where a physician had recommend-
ed Chekhov to drink goat's milk. Sept., in Moscow at rehearsals
of *Three Sisters.* 21 Sept, attended public performance and took
two curtain calls: generally satisfied with interpretation. Oct.,
returned to Yalta. Further deterioration in health.

1902 *The Bishop* published, Apr. Olga pregnant in Feb., had
a miscarriage at the end of Mar., and seriously ill for a fortnight
with peritonitis. Convalesence on Stanislavsky's estate at Lyubi-
movka. Aug., resigned from the Academy of Sciences over
Gorky's exclusion. Completed his last short story, *The Betrothed.*
Received Griboyedov Prize for *Three Sisters. The Cherry Orchard*
first mentioned in letter of 24 Dec.

1903 Approached by Diagilev with a request to edit *The World
of Art.* Completed three drafts of *The Cherry Orchard* between
Sept., and Oct. 4 Dec., moved to Moscow for Art Theatre production.

1904 17 Jan., premiere of *The Cherry Orchard:* Chekhov
summoned to the theatre despite being ill and speeches and
presentations made. 3 June, left with Knipper for the health
resort of Badenweiler in the Black Forest, on doctor's orders.
29 June, suffered the first of two heart attacks, and died at 3.00
a.m. on the morning of 2 July. 9 July, body interred in Novode-
vichy Cemetery, Moscow.

A Forced Declaration

or *The Sudden Death of a Horse*, or *The Magnanimity of the Russian People*
Written: 1876.
First production: 30 Feb. 1886 The Bat Th., Moscow.
First published: New Times, No. 4721, 22 Apr. 1889.
Translation: in Vera Gottlieb, *Chekhov and the Vaudeville* (Cambridge, 1982), p.197-9.

Two lovers are heading for the railway station in a cab, fleeing from the irate husband. They lash the cabman who, in turn, lashes his horse which, in turn, drops down dead. While the driver is sobbing over the corpse the husband catches them up and rewards the cabman with a hundred roubles. The driver declares that saving the count's honour is worth more than financial reward and is hoisted shoulder high by the appreciative crowd which has gathered.

Dishonourable Tragedians and Leprous Dramatists

'A terrible-awful-disgraceful desperate trrragedy. Many acts, more scenes.'
Written: 1884.
First published: in *The Alarm Clock,* No. 4, 1884.
Translation: in Vera Gottlieb, *Chekhov and the Vaudeville* (Cambridge, 1982), p.193-6.

The play opens with an epilogue in which a heart-rending male sits at a desk covered in blood. His head is a skull, his mouth is full of burning brimstone, and little green devils jump out of his nostrils smiling disdainfully. He dips his pen in lava stirred by witches and drinks burning oil while contemplating what to write next. Suddenly, an impresario appears in a clap of thunder demanding to know whether the play is ready. The scene shifts rapidly to a theatre and then to the palace of Charles XII, who complains about the plot of the play

*and consigns the playwright to the dungeons. In Acts 3 and 4
Stella, sister of the impresario, makes love to a young count. In
Acts 5 and 6 she escapes from prison, Charles XII orders virtue to
triumph over vice, the moon smiles, and so do the stars. All in
about three pages of text.*

On the High Road

'A dramatic study in one act'.
Written: 1884.
First London production: St. Martin's Th., 25 Jan. 1920 (with
    Cathleen Nesbitt as Marya, William Armstrong as Bortsov,
    and George Hayes as Merik).
First New York production: Civic Repertory Th., 14 Jan. 1929.
Revived: Key Th., New York, 20 Apr. 1961 (dir. Amnon Kabat-
    chnik); Half Moon Th., London, 26 Jan. 1982 (dir. Michael
    Batz).
First published: 1914.
Translations: in *Plays by Anton Tchekoff, Second Series,* trans.
    Julius West (New York, 1916); in *Plays from the Russian Vol.
    II,* trans. Constance Garnett (London, 1923); and in *Oxford
    Chekhov I.*

*The action of the play takes place at night in a public house on
a country road. Among the various tramps and rogues who have
come to the public house for warmth and shelter is a down-and-
out nobleman who implores the landlord to give him drink on
credit. From the conversation it transpires that the nobleman
took to drink because his wife deserted him on their wedding
day. By accident a lady seeks shelter from the rain in the public
house, and the unhappy drunkard recognizes her as his unfaithful
spouse. One of the visitors at the public house rushes upon her
with an axe, but he is held back. The dramatic study ends with
this unsuccessful attempt on the lady's life. This gloomy and
sordid play cannot, in my opinion, be allowed to be performed.*
    From the Censor's report rejecting the play, 20 Sept. 1885

On The High Road is in its main interest very much after the
fashion of Gorky's *The Lower Depths*, everything happening in a

wayside inn, where an assortment of various types of despondent and degenerate humanity encumber the floor. One is reminded that, as Gogol said, 'Russia is a wonderful country, but the fleas bite like dogs.' ... When it comes to the action, however, Chekhov is betrayed into the most threadbare old melodramatic story of a long-lost, unfaithful, but flagrantly well-to-do wife turning up accidentally. Chekhov among the Melvilles!

S.R.L[ittlewood], *Pall Mall Gazette,* 26 Jan. 1920

Swan Song

'A dramatic study in one act'.
Written: 1886-87.
First production: Korsh Th., Moscow, 19 Feb. 1888.
First London production: King's Th., Hammersmith, 17 Oct. 1928.
First New York production: Booth Th., 15 Apr. 1946.
Revived: Arts Th., London, 15 July 1942 (dir. Alec Clunes);
    Hampstead Th., 31 Aug. 1964 (dir. Anton Hatzinestoros).
First published: in *Season,* 1 (Moscow, 1887); and in full in
    Chekhov's *Plays* (St. Petersburg, 1897).
Translations: in *Plays by Anton Tchekoff,* trans. Marian Fell
    (New York, 1912); in *Plays from the Russian Vol. II,* trans.
    Constance Garnett (London, 1923); and in *Oxford Chekhov I.*

A two-hander set on the stage of a provincial theatre late at night following a benefit performance for Svetlovidov, an aged comic actor, who finds himself locked in, having fallen asleep, drunk, in his dressing room. Standing on the darkened stage he is suddenly startled by the 'ghost' of Nikita, an old prompter. Carried away on a wave of his own thwarted potential, Svetlovidov treats Nikita to a solo recitation consisting of snatches from leading tragic roles he has never played. The reflection which he contemplates in the 'mirror' provided by the admiring prompter fuels his maudlin sense of undervalued isolation, while the darkened auditorium puts him in mind of the grave and of a wasted life.

The Bear

Farce in one act.
Written: 1888.

First production: Korsh Th., Moscow, 28 Oct. 1888 (with
    dedicatee N.N. Solovtsov as Smirnov).
First London production: Kingsway Th., 14 May 1911.
First New York production: Washington Square Players, 24 May
    1915.
Revived: Kleines Th., Berlin, 12 Feb. 1905 (dir. Max Reinhardt);
    St. Martin's Th., 25 Jan. 1920; Everyman Th., Hampstead,
    24 May 1926 (dir. Nancy Price); Arts Th., London, 14 Oct.
    1948 (dir. Lucie Mannheim); Prince's Th., New York, 4 Apr.
    1949 (dir. Laurence Green).
First published: in *New Times,* 30 Aug. 1888.
Translations: by Roy Temple House (New York, 1909); Hilmar
    Baukhage (New York, 1915); in *Plays by Anton Tchekoff,
    Second Series,* trans. Julius West (New York, 1916); in *Plays
    from the Russian Vol. I,* trans. Constance Garnett (London,
    1923); in *The Brute and Other Farces by Anton Chekhov,*
    trans. Eric Bentley and Theodore Hoffman (New York,
    1958); in *Anton Chekhov: Plays,* trans. Elisaveta Fen
    (Harmondsworth, 1959); in *The Portable Chekhov,* ed.
    Avrahm Yarmolinsky (New York, 1947); and in *Oxford
    Chekhov I.*

---

*Smirnov, a middle-aged landowner, has made what amounts to a
forced entry into the drawing room of Popova, a dimpled widow,
who is in deep mourning and stubbornly refusing to pay off the
debt owed by her dead husband until her bailiff's return. The
bulk of the play consists of a quarrel between the two in which
each reveals a comic sense of bitterness at the way the opposite
sex has treated them. Having declared an aversion to men and
women respectively, they can only accept each other when she
behaves like a man (accepting his challenge to a duel) and he
behaves like a woman, in a 'sloppy, soft and sentimental' fashion.*

The Bear was quite an amusing little trifle in which Miss Dorothy
Massingham and Mr. Joseph A Dodd appeared as a widow who is
wooed with what military strategists would describe as 'the
utmost violence' by an elderly stranger, who, in the midst of
arrangements for fighting a duel with her, hugs her instead, without any strong protest on her part. It is, of course, the oldest
story in the world. Shakespeare's Richard and Anne, and Kath-
erine and Petruchio, have both their bearing on it. Still, it was

bright and astonishingly definite in its humour, though Miss Massingham was a little too tall, and did not quite suggest the undercurrent of conscious allurement.

S.R.L[ittlewood], *Pall Mall Gazette,* 26 Jan. 1920

Recently we saw [Zinaida Raikh] in *The Lady of the Camellias.* The dramatic character of Marguerite Gautier which had been revealed by her lyrically – all of those half-shades, pauses, the sad play of glances, the voice full of feeling, the hidden feelings – the more hidden, the dearer they were to her. And lo and behold! – maybe it is a risky comparison – but there appeared Marguerite's younger sister. The very same lyricism: half-shades, pauses, play of glances, hidden feelings. But only within the plane of a comedy. It is as if the younger sister were teasing the older one. . . . Everything that there is of a French element, of a Maupassant element, of 'winking', of the slyly ironical in the words 'young widow' opens up in the presentation of Popova. 'The young widow!' . . . this is a whole culture . . . a real social type . . . She hides [vice], but she hides it gracefully, which means she is hiding and showing it, and in this is the whole art: to hide so that it can be seen, otherwise there is no play. What kind of young widow is she? She is also a hypocrite, but hypocrisy is here playing with open cards, that is to say – the revealing of the method.

Yu. Yuzovsky in Meyerhold's production of 1935
quoted in Vera Gottlieb, *Chekhov and the Vaudeville*
(Cambridge, 1982), p.52

The Proposal

Farce in one act.
Written: 1888-89.
First production: Artists' Club, St. Petersburg, 12 Apr. 1889.
First London production: Kingsway Th., Dec. 1931.
First New York production: Lindsey Th., 18 Sept. 1945 (dir. Paul Hardmuth).
Revived: Meyerhold Th., Moscow, 25 Mar. 1935; Arts Th., London, 26 Aug. 1942 (dir. Alec Clunes); New Theatre, London, 10 Feb. 1949 (dir. Laurence Olivier); Roundabout Th., New York, 20 Dec. 1971 (dir. Sterling Jensen).
First published: in *New Times,* 3 May 1889.
Translations: by W.H.H. Chambers in *The Drama: its History,*

Literature, and Influence on Civilization Vol. XVIII (London, 1903); trans. Hilmar Bakhage and Barrett H. Clark (New York, 1914); in *Plays by Anton Tchekoff, Second Series,* trans. Julius West (New York, 1916); in *Plays from the Russian Vol. I,* trans. Constance Garnett (London, 1923); in *Anton Chekhov: Plays,* trans. Elisaveta Fen (Harmondsworth, 1959); in *The Brute, and Other Farces by Anton Chekhov,* trans. Eric Bentley and Theodore Hoffman (New York, 1958); and in *Oxford Chekhov I.*

Lomov is a hefty and well-nourished hypochondriac who suffers from nervous palpitations. Having decided that marriage is a possible cure for his complaint, he has called at Chubukov's country house to request permission to court his daughter Natasha. The father at first assumes he has come to borrow money but then, delightedly learning the purpose of his visit, informs his daughter, offstage, merely that 'a buyer has come for the goods'. Misunderstanding the purpose of his visit, Natasha taunts Lomov as they begin to quarrel about who owns a piece of land adjoining their estates. Chubukov eventually joins in, before Lomov, whose heart is feeling the strain, staggers from the scene. Chubukov inadvertently reveals why he called in the first place, and Natasha hysterically demands that he be brought back. The final scene begins with a now contrite and eager Natasha attempting to prompt the exhausted Lomov into proposing. He inevitably misunderstands her and a second quarrel ensues, Chubukov insulting Lomov to the point where the latter faints aways and is taken for dead. When he begins to show signs of reviving, Chubukov gratefully seizes the chance to seal an engagement between the dazed Lomov and his daughter, whereupon they resume their quarrel.

Meyerhold's directorial methods emerged with particular sharpness in *The Proposal.* There, for example, developing a device discovered in *The Magnanimous Cuckold* and then shown in a transformed manner in *The Forest,* Meyerhold builds a whole series of moments on a materialization of the text and situation through the way properties are handled. The property, lacking any relationship to the text, achieves the status of some form of 'symbol' and, in addition, as an expression of an emotional condition. The serviette which Lomov and Natalya Stepanovna tear to shreds between the two of them . . . 'symbolizes' the subject of their embittered quarrel – the Volovy Meadows. Lomov's relationship to the two dogs Ugaday and Otkatay is emphasized by the way he handles his top hat and his soft hat and so on.

A. Fevralsky, *Sovetsky Teatr,* Nos. 2-3 (1935)

The Wedding

Play in one act.
Written: 1889.
First recorded production: Hunting Club, Moscow, 28 Nov.
   1900 (dir. N.N. Arbatov).
First London production: Russian Exhibition, Grafton Galleries,
   May 1917 (dir. Nigel Playfair).
First New York production: New York City Center Th., 5 Feb.
   1948.
Revived: St. Martin's Th., London, 25 Jan. 1920; Mansurov
   Studio, Moscow, Sept. 1920 (dir. E. Vakhtangov); Alexandrin-
   sky Th., 1 May 1902 (dir. M.E. Yergenyev); Moscow Art
   Theatre Studio, Sept. 1921 (dir. E. Vakhtangov); Old Vic,
   London, 13 Mar. 1951 (dir. George Devine); Key Th., New
   York, 20 Apr. 1961 (dir. Anton Kabatchnik).
First published: Oct. 1890.
Translations: in *Five Russian Plays,* trans. C.E. Bechhofer (New
   York, 1916); in *Plays by Anton Chekoff, Second Series,*
   trans. Julius West (New York, 1916); in *Plays from the
   Russian, Vol. II,* trans. Constance Garnett (London, 1923);
   in *The Brute, and Other Farces by Anton Chekhov,* trans. Eric
   Bentley and Theodore Hoffman (New York, 1958); and in
   Oxford Chekhov I.

*A brightly-lit room in a second-rate restaurant. Against a back-
ground of music, the guests engage in flirtations, quarrels, and
complaints. The bride's mother expresses indignation at the fact
that a 'distinguished guest' can't be found for love nor money. A
langorous female guest announces the theme of the play when she
declares she is bored to suffocation and, quoting Lermontov, says
she feels like a sailing ship and 'seeks a storm'. After a faltering
speech from a male visitor, a 'distinguished guest' is ushered in*

and passed off as a 'general', but turns out to be an unsuspecting, good-natured eccentric – a retired sea-captain who possesses a one-track mind which runs on ships and patterns of command. Soon the guests are in the middle of a verbal storm as the captain reminisces enthusiastically and shouts orders. Disabused, the captain makes a dignified exit, while the proceedings carry on as best they can.

'Have you ever staged Chekhov?' 'Some of his stories, yes, not his big plays. Several years ago we thought of presenting his *Wedding*.' 'We did it at school.' 'Well?' 'It was fun rehearsing it.' 'Then you think a wedding is a merry occasion?' 'It seems so!' 'Did Chekhov think so too?' 'No, I don't think he did.' 'Then who's right? You or Chekhov?'

Strictly speaking, Vakhtangov did not expect me to answer this complicated question and I, believing it best to pretend I was thinking, said nothing.

'Perhaps it's no life at all the way they live in Chekhov's plays', Vakhtangov continued. 'Everybody dances, everybody makes merry celebrating the wedding, everything is "as it should be", even a "general" has been "hired", but that's not life. They think they live, but in reality someone is pulling the strings and telling them: "That's how it should be". They dance, quarrel, make up, drink, eat, love, hate, buy, sell'.

'But isn't that mysticism?' I asked, somewhat hesitantly. 'What is?' 'The idea that Chekhov's characters are puppets.' 'No, it's one of the possible interpretations of the real theatrical significance of Chekhov's plays', Vakhtangov answered with unexpected joviality and began humming some old quadrille.

Nikolai Gorchakov, *The Vakhtangov School of Stage Art*
(Moscow, n.d.), p.29-30

Tatyana Repina

Drama in one act.
Written: 1889.
No recorded performance. First published: 1889.
Translations: in *Anton Tchekhov: Literary and Theatrical Reminiscences,* ed. S.S. Koteliansky (London, 1927); in *Tchekhov's Plays and Stories,* trans. S.S. Koteliansky (London, 1967); and in *Oxford Chekhov I.*

A continuation of the play Tatyana Repina *(1886) written by Chekhov's friend and publisher A.S. Suvorin, and based on the story of the actress E.P. Kadmina, who took poison on stage to punish her faithless lover. Chekhov's play is set in a cathedral and lasts the length of the Orthodox marriage service in which one Sabinin is being united with the dead Repina's rival in love, Vera Olenina. At the end of the service a 'Woman in Black', whom Olenina identifies as a reincarnation of Repina, poisons herself in the name of all women and in protest at the injustices of the world. Most of the play consists of comic 'montage' effects as Chekhov cuts between the solemn ritual and the comments of members of the joking, chatting congregation.*

Anton was a great connoisseur of church literature. He knew the Bible perfectly, he knew it from his early childhood; he was also very fond of the directness and of the florid unusual words of the hymns, many of which he knew by heart. He also had a small library of church ritual and service books. . . . In Anton's *Tatyana Riepin* the action takes place in church. At that time the idea was quite unusual, and of course perfectly inadmissible from the point of view of the censor. . . . The whole interest of Anton's play centres in the marriage ceremony. . . . The marriage ritual is fully adhered to in the play, with the reading of the New Testament and all the other particulars.

Michael Chekhov (Anton's brother), quoted in *Tchekhov's Plays and Stories,* trans. S.S. Koteliansky (London, 1967), p.175-6

The contrast with Suvorin's play exists at every level. Whereas Suvorin's play is composed of lengthy, unmotivated, and high-flown monologues, Chekhov's characters speak in short sentences, in ordinary speech, with the dialogue constructed out of inter-jections, irrelevancies, association of ideas, and rapid responses. Individuals are picked out as if by a camera panning across a crowd, pausing, and then passing on, or cutting rapidly. . . . In this way, the structure of the play is created partly by Chekhov's increasingly frequent use of juxtaposition – the solemnity of the wedding ritual, the prayers and the singing of the choir are juxtaposed throughout the play with the joking and chatting public and – as often in Chekhov's plays – one is used to comment, sometimes comically, on the other. . . . Thus Chekhov's cathedral is turned into a performance space, the wedding into a public ritual, and the characters into a mixture of actors and audience; as a result, the reader is given a constantly shifting perspective which then governs the objective view of the whole scene, and which enables him to see the comic in juxtaposition with the dramatic, and those moments where the 'dramatic' is, in fact, quite deliberately shown as 'melodramatic'.

Vera Gottlieb, *Chekhov and the Vaudeville* (Cambridge, 1982), p.143-5

A Tragedian despite Himself

'From Life at a Summer Dacha. A Jest in One Act'.
Written: 1889–90.
First production: German Club, St. Petersburg, 1 Oct. 1989 (dir. A. Dmitriev).
First New York production: Majestic Th., 1935 (with Michael Chekhov).
First published: June 1889.
Translations: in *Plays by Anton Tchekoff, Second Series,* trans. Julius West (New York, 1916); as *An Unwilling Martyr,* in *Plays from the Russian Vol. II* (London, 1923); trans. Olive Frances Murphy, in *Poet Lore, XXXIII* (Boston, 1922); as *Summer in the Country* in *The Brute, and Other Farces by Anton Chekhov,* trans. Eric Bentley and Theodore Hoffman (New York, 1958); and as *A Tragic Role* in *Oxford Chekhov I.*

Virtually a monologue spoken by Tolkachov, a family man, whose wife and children have joined the summer migration to dachas at Corpse Creek. He is having to commute to his Petersburg office in the heat of the day, as well as perform marathon shopping errands for his family and friends, and has just arrived at his friend Murashkin's flat weighed down with parcels. Appearing to be contemplating suicide, he embarks on a litany of complaint which forms the central speech of the play and which concludes with the plea that, as a living being, he wants . . . Life! It also becomes clear that, either Murashkin hasn't been listening, or doesn't take his friend's complaints seriously, for he insensitively asks if he wouldn't mind carrying a few packages to a friend who also happens to be summering at Corpse Creek. Tolkachov pursues Murashkin round the room screaming for blood.

The Anniversary

'Joke' in one act.

Written: 1891.

First production: Soc. of Art and Literature, Moscow, 20 Nov. 1900.

First London production: Kingsway Th., Dec. 1931.

First New York production: Key Th., 20 Apr. 1961 (dir. Amnon Kabatchnik).

Revived: Fellowship of the New Drama, Kherson, 17 Dec. 1903 (dir. V.E. Meyerhold); Meyerhold Th., Moscow, 25 Mar. 1935.

First published: May 1892; revised version in *Collected Works,* 2nd ed., VII (St. Petersburg, 1903).

Translation: as *The Jubilee,* trans. Olive Frances Murphy, in *Poet Lore, XXXI* (Boston, 1920); in *Five Russian Plays,* trans. C.E. Bechhofer (New York, 1916); in *Plays by Anton Tchekoff, Second Series,* trans. Julius West (New York, 1916); in *Plays from the Russian, Vol. II,* trans. Constance Garnett (London, 1923); in *Anton Chekhov: Plays,* trans. Elisaveta Fen (Harmondsworth, 1959); as *The Celebration* in *The Brute, and Other Farces by Anton Chekhov,* trans. Eric Bentley and Theodore Hoffman (New York, 1958); and in *Oxford Chekhov I.*

It is the fifteenth anniversary of the founding of the Mutual Credit Bank in the town of N. In the chairman's office the misogynist book-keeper Khirin is putting the finishing touches to his boss, Shipuchin's, speech to the shareholders. The male world of business is invaded, first by Shipuchin's wife, back from the country with her head full of romance and, secondly, by one Merchutkina, seeking redress for her husband's wrongful dismissal. While Merchutkina pleads to be given the money deducted from her husband's final pay packet and Mrs. Shipuchin recounts her sister's romantic goings-on, Khirin is trying to finalize the speech as well as do his accounts. Invited by Shipuchin to 'get rid of' Merchutkina, Khirin rounds on Mrs. Shipuchin and threatens to 'slit the throats' of all women. A chase follows, which ends with Mrs. Shipuchin fainting and Merchutkina collapsing.

The people in Chekhov's vaudeville are strange enough; in Meyerhold's production lunatics are on the loose. The nine fainting fits of the vaudeville are points where madness reaches its apotheosis. The insanity of each character reaches a crescendo until each passes out and falls flat on his/her back to the music of Strauss. In Chekhov, these are just amusing people; Meyerhold inflates the comic aspect to hyperbolical proportions so that on stage we have crackpots. To each belongs his or her own point of craziness. Shipuchin has illusions of grandeur; Merchutkina has the obsession with 24 roubles 36 kopecks; Khirin is fixed on his mistrust; Tatyana is fixated in eroticism. . . . We know that Khirin has gone for his wife and sister-in-law with a knife. Fair enough. In front of us here we have an insane person peering suspiciously around him. His head is huddled in a cloth because he believes himself to be ill . . . he seems to talk to himself, smiles a madman's smile as if to say, just you wait, something awful's going to happen in a minute. In the play, Khirin yells spitefully at Tatyana Alekseyevna 'Get out!' In the production he does this with visible pleasure. He draws a revolver, which is not in Chekhov's play, and with a blissful smile loads it bullet by bullet, slowly, lapping it up. He pursues those present with the revolver and his eyes are alight with glee. It's as if he's been awaiting this opportunity for years. With what passion he tears Shipuchin's speech to shreds. Nobody would have been surprised if, for no particular reason, he had simply set fire to the whole bank.

Yu. Yuzovsky, *Spektakly i P'esy* (Moscow, 1935), p.314-5

The Night before Judgement

Unfinished one-act play.
Written: 1890s.
No recorded performance.
First published: in *Collected Works Vol. XII* (Moscow, 1944-51).
Translations: trans. Anna Heifetz, in *American Mercury LXIII*,
    No. 276 (New York, 1946); and in *Oxford Chekhov I*.

Three people are in transit through a 'hellish' blizzard and have arrived at a bug-infested inn. They are Zaitsev, a young man travelling to the town where he is due to be tried next day for attempted murder, bigamy, and forgery; and the elderly Gusev, the judge destined to try Zaitsev's case, who is also heading for the town with his young wife Zina. Zaitsev engages in a serio-comic conversation with his revolver, first contemplating suicide, then snuggling down with the weapon in bed, while Zina is awakened in the adjoining room by bedbugs. Zaitsev masquerades as a doctor and persuades the sceptical Gusev to let him examine his wife in private, and while Gusev is out of the room Zina invites Zaitsev to embrace her. The play breaks off at a point where Zaitsev has formulated a bogus prescription comprising two drams of 'sic transit', an ounce of 'gloria mundi', and two grammes of 'aquae distillatae' powder to be taken in boiled water.

On the Harmfulness of Tobacco

Stage monologue in one act.
Written: 1886.
No first performance recorded.
First London production: Hampstead Th., 31 Aug. 1964 (dir. Anton Hatzinestoros).
First New York production: City Center, 5 Feb. 1948.
Revived: Roundabout Th., New York, 20 Dec. 1971 (dir. Nancy Roberts).
First published: Petersburg Gazette, 17 Feb. 1886, and in *Collected Works, XIV* (1903);
Translations: as *The Tobacco Evil*, trans. Henry James Forman, in *Theatre Arts Magazine, VII* (New York, 1922); in *Anton Tchekhov: Literary and Theatrical Reminiscences*, ed. S.S. Koteliansky (London, 1927); in *The Plays of Anton Chekhov*, trans. Constance Garnett (New York, 1946); in *The Brute, and Other Farces by Anton Chekhov*, trans. Eric Bentley and Theodore Hoffman (New York, 1958); and as *Smoking is Bad for You*, in *Oxford Chekhov I.*

Ivan Ivanovich Nyukhin (Sniffer), described as 'his wife's husband', is addressing a provincial audience on 'The Harmfulness of Tobacco'. The theme has been chosen for him by his spouse, and there is a Freudian subtext to his monologue on the dangers of inhaling tobacco or snuff. Even the bedbugs can't kick the habit and are breeding like mad. His wife, it appears, is trying to put a stop to it by running a school for female boarders in which Nyukhin functions as an emasculated 'matron' and is forced to eat the leftovers. In daring to depart from his text in an attempt to get members of the audience interested in meeting his thirteen daughters, Nyukhin is brought sharply back to his theme when he notices 'her' standing in the wings.

Platonov

Untitled play in four acts.
Written: c.1880–81 (manuscript acquired by Soviet State Literary Archive in 1920).
First production: Germany, early 1928.
First London production: Royal Court Th., 13 Oct. 1960 (dir. George Devine and John Blatchley; des. Richard Negri; with Rex Harrison).
Revived: Vakhtangov Th., Moscow, 31 Jan. 1960 (dir. A. Remizova); Théâtre National Populaire, 8 Nov. 1956 (dir. Jean Vilar); Piccolo Teatro, Milan, 1959 (dir. Giorgio Strehler).
First published: 1923
Translations: incomplete, as *That Worthless Fellow Platonov,* trans. John Cournos (London, 1930); as *Don Juan (in the Russian Manner),* trans. Basil Ashmore (London, 1952); as *A Country Scandal,* adapted by Alex Szogyi (New York, 1960); trans. Dmitri Makaroff (London, 1961); trans. David Magarshack (London, 1964); and in *Oxford Chekhov II.*

The action of this tragi-farce about love, 'platonic' and otherwise, unfolds on the Voynitsev estate in Southern Russia and principally involves Platonov, a local schoolmaster of 27, his wife Sasha, and the other women in his life – the widowed estate owner Anna Voynitseva, her daughter-in-law Sofya, and Marya Grekova, a young intellectual with scientific interests. At a social gathering in the Voynitseva manor house, Platonov and Anna establish a mutual tone of immoral freemasonry while he proceeds to humiliate Grekova in public and pays scant attention to his own wife. But his feelings for Sofya are reawakened after an interval of five years, during which she has married someone else, and she starts to hope that this might be the beginning of a 'new life'. The scene shifts to a schoolhouse in a forest clearing, where Osip, a violent horse thief employed by Voynitseva, witnesses a love duet between his employer and Platonov and, in a fit of jealousy, vows to kill him. Sasha tries to commit suicide by laying herself across the railway track, but is saved by Osip. The third act opens three weeks later with Sofya reproaching Platonov for failing to run away with her, while a clerk delivers a magistrate's summons from Grekova for the earlier insult. Osip arrives, scuffles with Platonov, and succeeds in stabbing him in the arm. The fourth act shifts to a study in the Voynitseva house: Platonov has again failed to keep his appointment with Sofya, and is informed that his wife has unsuccessfully tried to kill herself by eating matches. Grekova, who has earlier received a touching note from Platonov, arrives with declarations of love. As Platonov's delirium (a consequence of his wound) intensifies, Sofya enters and shoots him at the second attempt. A doctor, Triletsky, declares that life amounts to little more than a kopeck.

If anyone still lives who needs proof of Chekhov's genius, let him go and see *Platonov*. This is the master's first play, composed when he was twenty-one. It makes a singular impression; as if a Russian novel of country life had been dramatized by Georges Feydeau and then handed over to Chekhov for total rewriting. . . .

Here are the theatrical first fruits of Chekhov's lifelong curiosity about the symptoms and causes of human boredom. Drunk or sober, the characters address each other with disastrous candour. They change the subject on impulse, almost by free association, and they have the Chekhovian (or perhaps the Russian) habit of taking calamities lightly and trivialities tragically. With them, elation and suicidal gloom are split seconds apart.

In the midst of this provincial desolation squirms Platonov, who must be regarded as one of the great comic creations of the last hundred years. . . . In the course of the play Platonov meshes limbs with a sexy widow and an idealistic young wife; he also insults a local blue-stocking so challengingly that she mistakes insult for love. His three liaisons ultimately collide, and in their collision, which involves a great slamming and locking and bursting open of doors, resides what we may call the Feydeau element of the plot.

It is here that Rex Harrison, as Platonov, comes into his own. Edgy and tentative in the first expository act, he now expands and relaxes. This beared satyr, febrile and wild-eyed, rides a perfect switchback from euphoria to misery. He makes the farce funny, by impeccable timing, and touching, an instant later, by his ability to convert querulous complaints into emotional assets. We almost pity the cad, leering and whining though he usually is. He even looks Slavic; I shall not soon forget the scene in which he rises at dawn with a hangover, automatically downs a vodka, and pauses shortly thereafter, stricken by a genuine uncertainty, to ask himself: 'Did I have a drink just then?' . . . It is an indication of the production's general success that it ends, in the midst of laughter, with a thoroughly convincing death. A death, moreover, that happens on a hot, rainy morning. In Chekhov's plays even the weather is Chekhovian.

Kenneth Tynan, *Tynan Right and Left* (London, 1967), p.39-41

Ivanov

Drama in four acts.
Written: 1887.
First production: Fellowship of Russian Actors, Saratov, Nov. 1887 (dir. V.N. Andreyev-Burlak).
Revived (revised version): Aleksandrinsky Theatre, St. Petersburg, 31 Jan. 1889 (dir. F.A. Fyodorov-Yurkovsky); Moscow Art Th., 20 Oct. 1904 (dir. V.I. Nemirovich-Danchenko; des. V.A. Simov).
First London production: Duke of York's Th., 6 Dec. 1925 (dir. F. Komissarzhevsky; with Robert Farquharson as Ivanov and Jeanne de Casalis as Anna).
Revived: Arts Th., 20 Apr. 1950 (dir. John Fernald; with Michael Hordern); Phoenix Th., 30 Sept. 1965 (dir. John Gielgud); Aldwych Th., 2 Sept. 1976 (dir. David Jones; des. William Dudley; with John Wood as Ivanov); Old Vic, 14 Aug. 1978 (dir. Toby Robertson; des. Robin Archer; with Derek Jacobi as Ivanov).
First New York production: Jolson's 59th St. Th., 27 Nov. 1923.
Revived: Renata Th., July 1958 (dir. William Ball).
First published: Jan. 1888.
Translations: in *Plays by Anton Tchekoff,* trans. Marian Fell (New York, 1912); in *Plays from the Russian Vol. II,* trans. Constance Garnett (London, 1923); in *Plays by Anton Chekhov,* trans. Elisaveta Fen (Harmondsworth, 1959); in *Six Plays of Chekhov,* versions by Robert W. Corrigan (New York, 1962); in *Chekhov: the Major Plays* trans. Ann Dunnigan (New York, 1964); and in *Oxford Chekhov II.*

In the past Ivanov has been an active and enlightened farmer and administrator, but the task has proved too much for him: his estate has run into debt and Ivanov has become introspective, nerve-

ridden, and joyless. In his youth he married the daughter of a Jewish family who, out of love for him, reneged on her faith, and has been christened Anna. Now neglected, she is dying of tuberculosis while her bored husband seeks the solace of others' company on the estate of his friend and neighbour Lebedev, whose daughter Sasha wants to 'save' him. During Sasha's birthday party, Ivanov is a topic of scandal and rumour, but the gossip is interrupted by his arrival in company with his uncle, Count Shabelsky, and his relative Borkin with, unknown to him, Anna and Lvov, a doctor contemptuous of Ivanov, in hot pursuit. Sasha listens to Ivanov's disquisition on the state of his own mind before declaring she loves him: he decides to clutch at this straw, but their embrace is witnessed by Anna, whose condition soon worsens. Discovering Ivanov in Sasha's company yet again, Anna calls him a liar: he first calls her 'Jewess!', then says she'll soon be dead anyway, before collapsing in a fit of self-reproach. In the interval of a year between the third and fourth acts Anna has died and Ivanov is marrying Sasha. He arrives at the Lebedev's dressed for the ceremony – but with a pistol in his pocket, declaring he wants to call the whole thing off. Struck by the farcical absurdity of the subsequent discussion, Ivanov says he feels his youthful energy returning and, to prove it, runs aside and shoots himself.

I wrote the play by chance, after a single conversation with Korsh [owner of the Korsh Theatre in Moscow]. I went to bed, thought up a theme and wrote. I took two weeks over it or, more truly, ten days. . . . I can't judge the merits of the play. It's turned out suspiciously on the short side. Everyone likes it. Korsh hasn't found a single mistake or fault as far as its stageworthiness is concerned. . . . It's my first play, *ergo* there are bound to be mistakes. The plot is complicated and quite clear. I conclude every act like my short stories, leading the action along quietly and peacefully, then punching the spectator in the face at the end. All my energy has gone into a few scenes which are truly powerful and vivid, but the bridge passages which connect them are insignificant, pale, and cliché-ridden. All the same, I'm pleased; no matter how bad the play may be I have created a type which has literary significance, and a part which only a talent like Davydov [of the Aleksandrinsky Theatre, St. Petersburg] could play, a part in which an actor can stretch his wings and display his ability.

Chekhov, letter to his brother Alexander, 10–12 Oct. 1887

Contemporary dramatists stuff their plays with angels, scoundrels and fools exclusively — try and find these elements in the whole of Russia! You may find some but not in the extreme forms which dramatists seem to find necessary. I wanted to be original and not bring on a single villain, or a single angel (although I couldn't keep out the fools)...

Chekhov, letter to his brother Alexander, 24 Oct. 1887

I've just received your letter. You say the absence of Sasha at the end of Act IV is glaringly obvious. So it has to be. Let the audience note that Sasha isn't there. You insist on her appearing; that the laws of the theatre demand it. All right, let her come on, but what is she to say? What are her lines to be? Unmarried women like her (she's not a young girl but an unmarried woman) can't talk and oughtn't to. The earlier Sasha could talk and was likeable but the new one will only irritate the audience if she comes on. She can't possibly throw herself on Ivanov's neck and say 'I love you!' She doesn't love him and has already said as much... You say there isn't a single woman and that this makes the ending dry. I agree. Only two women could appear at the end to stand up for Ivanov, who actually loved him: his mother and the Jewish girl. But as they're both dead there can be no question of it. He's an orphan and he can damned well stay orphaned.

Chekhov, letter to A.S. Suvorin, 23 Dec. 1888

The director considers Ivanov a superfluous person in the Turgenev manner. Savina asks why Ivanov is a swine. You write, 'Ivanov must be given something to make it apparent why two women cling to him and why he is a swine and why the doctor is a great man'. If all three of you have understood me in this fashion then this means that my *Ivanov* is no good at all. . . .

I understand my heroes thus: Ivanov is a nobleman, a university man, with nothing remarkable about him. He is easily excitable, inclined to be carried away, fiery in spirit, honest and upright like the majority of well-brought-up members of the gentry. He has lived on his estate and served as a member of the regional council. What he's done and how he's behaved, what amuses him and keeps him occupied is evident from the following words of his addressed to the doctor (Act I Scene 5): 'Don't marry a Jew or a psychopath or a bluestocking . . . don't take on thousands single-handed, don't tilt against windmills or beat your head against brick walls, and God preserve you from all kinds of rational farming, experimental schools and wild speech-making'. That's what his past has been. Sarah, who was witness to his rational farming and other activities, says to the doctor: 'He's a remarkable man, doctor, and I only regret that you didn't know him two or three years ago. Now he is grumpy and silent and doesn't do anything, but previously . . . what a charmer!' . . .

Finding themselves in a position like this, people with bad consciences and narrow outlooks usually place all the blame on circumstances and enrol in the ranks of superfluous people and Hamlets and comfort themselves with that. But Ivanov is a direct person and openly announces in public to the doctor that he doesn't understand himself. . . . That he generally doesn't understand himself can be seen from the long monologue in Act 3 where, facing the audience, he confesses and even bursts into tears!

The change which has taken place in him insults his sense of propriety. He seeks the causes of this outside himself and can't find them; so he searches within himself and finds only a vague feeling of guilt. This is a Russian feeling. . . . To exhaustion, boredom, and the feeling of guilt add still another enemy. Loneliness. If Ivanov had been an official, a priest, an actor, a professor, he'd have got used to things. But he lives on an estate. It's out in the wilds. People there are either card-players or drunkards, or such as the doctor. They couldn't care less about his feelings and the changes in them. He is alone. . . .

Now for the fifth enemy. Ivanov is exhausted, doesn't understand himself, but life won't concern itself with this. It makes its own legitimate demands and he — whether he likes it or not — has to resolve the problem. His sick wife is a problem, his pile of debts is a problem, he's got Sasha round his neck and that's a problem. . . . Such as Ivanov do not resolve problems but collapse under their weight. They become confused, make despairing gestures, have attacks of nerves, complain, do stupid things and finally, give way to their depraved, neurotic spinelessness, feel the ground give way beneath them and collapse into the ranks of the 'misunderstood' and the 'broken-down'. . . .

So as not to tire you to the point of collapse, I'll move on to Dr. Lvov. He is the type of the honest, upright, hot-headed but narrow-minded and compartmentalized individual. Clever people say of him 'He's stupid, but he's honest'. Everything which is like breadth of vision or straightforward feeling is alien to Lvov. He is a walking cliché, tendentiousness personified. He regards everything and everyone through blinkers and his judgements are all preformed. . . . In every well-to-do peasant he saw an exploiter and in Ivanov – whom he failed to understand – he saw a swine straightaway. The man has a sick wife, he visits a rich female neighbour – what else can he be? . . . He never feels any pangs of conscience – after all he's an 'honest worker' here to set 'the forces of reaction' by the ears. Such people are necessary and are mostly likeable. To caricature them, if only in the interests of the stage, is dishonest and pointless. . . .

Now, about the women. What are they in love for? Sarah loves Ivanov because he's a decent man, because he has enthusiasm, sparkle, and speaks as heatedly as Lvov. She loves him as long as he's exciting and interesting, but when she thinks he's fading before her eyes and losing these definite qualities, she no longer understands him and speaks out bluntly and sharply at the end of Act 3.

Sasha is a modern young woman. She is well-educated, intelligent, honest, and so forth. As the only big fish in a small pond she singles out 35-year-old Ivanov. He's the best of the bunch. She's known him since she was a small child and could observe all his activities at close range at a time when he wasn't played-out. He's her father's friend. . . .

She's the sort of woman who loves men when they're going downhill. As soon as Ivanov begins to feel downcast – she's there. It's the moment she's been waiting for. What a noble, sacred task she now has! She'll resurrect the fallen, stand him on his own feet, give him happiness. It's not Ivanov she loves but this mission. . . . Sasha doesn't realize that life is not like it is in novels. She . . . works at him for a whole year but instead of showing any signs of life he sinks down further and further.

Chekhov, letter to A.S. Suvorin, 30 Dec. 1888

You say that I shouldn't have taken Ivanov 'ready-made'. . . . If my Ivanov isn't clear to everyone then this is because all four acts have been done by an incompetent hand, and not at all because I have taken my hero 'ready-made'. Tolstoy's heroes are taken 'ready-made'; their past and their features are unknown, are guessed at through hints, but surely you wouldn't say that these characters don't satisfy you. . . . The contours of my Ivanov are correctly given, he is begun as he needs to be and my instinct doesn't detect anything false; however, the shading is poor and because of this you suspect the outline.

The women in my play are not essential. One of the chief problems was how to prevent the women from becoming the focus of attention, when this belongs elsewhere. If I have succeeded in making them beautiful, then I consider my task is done as far as they are concerned. Women contribute to the downfall of Ivanov. So what? Surely it isn't necessary to embark on a long explanation of their involvement, which has already been understood and treated at length by others a thousand times before me.

Chekhov, letter to Suvorin, 8 Feb. 1889

Last night [Chekhov] rang the curtain down on the spectacle of a wife fainting to discover a neighbour's buxom daughter in her husband's arms. And to close the piece he solved his problem by recourse to a pistol shot and a suicide, a device that is no solution at all and yet is one that, Mr. Galsworthy will tell you, never fails to end a play.

Chekhov may have been a little fustian and shop worn in spots, but he had all the talent of the company from Moscow working for him. Katchaloff played the title role of a wastrel and characterless country gentleman who had married a Jewess only to find her parents promptly disinheriting her, and who at the opening of the play is soothing his self-centred soul by arousing a romantic and motherly interest in the breast of his neighbour's daughter.

Katchaloff did not have an opportunity to show his audience the gradual disintegration of a man's character in his role of Ivanov, for Chekhov was not dramatist enough in his earlier days to develop this process. One beheld from the outset a characterless and colourful man who remained static in his spiritual state through to the end. It was Katchaloff's and not Chekhov's play. He did with it everything an actor might do to coerce drama from a clumsy piece. . . . Stanislavsky, as a lascivious and senile count enamored of a country-side widow, did a beautiful piece of clowning in the manner of twenty years ago, while Leonidoff played to the richly burlesqued hilt the part of a drunken and engaging overseer. . . .

L.S., *The World*, New York, 28 Nov. 1923

What a part Nicholas Ivanoff is to play! He is a modern Russian (a very Russian) Hamlet; a lost soul that has broken its wings in an attempt to soar above the commonplace futility of life. And as it is Russian life of the 'eighties, laced with vodka and too much tea, you can imagine how futile it is.

Chekhov is the laureate of futility. All his characters are dimly conscious that they are futile. They rebel incessantly against the boredom of life. But they have not the power to live fully because they have not the will. In the play . . . the hero has broken his back in attempting too much in life. . . . Robert Farquharson . . . has never done anything better than his Ivanov, but it would be idle to pretend that he really succeeded in expressing all that could be made of the part. He gave us only the husk of the character, and seldom realized the terrible struggle in the stricken man's mind. . . . But the greatest praise must be given to Komisarjevsky for his production of this strange, repulsive and yet tremendously interesting play.

E.A.B., *Daily News*, London, 8 Dec. 1925

It is a play that already shows the Tchehovian melancholy and poetic shimmer, but fails in totality through its inability to win sympathy for its self-pitying hero, Ivanov: a character who, blundering in inexplicable dejection of mind between an ailing wife and radiant young worshipper, can find no solution but self-destruction to his own incapability of happiness. This character Michael Hordern played with chiselled distinction, but even with such an actor Tchehov's Hamlet-of-the-Steppes failed fully to move us.

Audrey Williamson, *Theatre of Two Decades* (London, 1951), p.204

The mixture of comedy and tragedy, which later on become blended indistinguishably, is here crude and lumpy. . . . Moreover, the comedy is generally broader than in the later comedies, harking back rather to the style of Chekhov's early one-act farces. . . . So we have in effect a late-Chekhov plot-outline treated in an early Chekhov way. . . . Perhaps the effect of this is intensified somewhat by the present production. Sir John [Gielgud] himself is splendid in Ivanov's quieter moments of sad self-realization — the passages, in fact, where Ivanov is closest to Uncle Vanya, but one cannot feel that he is altogether with the character when called on for bouts of uncontrollable passion. . . . Arguably there should be a perceptible undercurrent of hysteria and desperation running through the whole role which Sir John has not quite succeeded in capturing.

John Russell Taylor, *Plays and Players*, Dec. 1965, p.33

The Wood Demon

Comedy in four acts.
Written: 1889.
First production: Abramova Th., Moscow, 27 Dec. 1889.
First London production: Wimbledon Th., 8 Apr. 1974 (dir
   David Giles; with Ian McKellan as Khrushchev).
First published: 1890.
Translations: in *Anton Chekhov: Plays and Stories,* trans. S.S.
   Koteliansky (London, 1967); in *Six Plays of Chekhov,* versions
   by Robert W. Corrigan (New York, 1962); and in *Oxford
   Chekhov III.*

Alexander Serebryakov, a retired professor of literature, has
moved from the city with his young second wife, Yelena, to live
on the Voynitsky estate with his brother-in-law George and
Sonya, Serebryakov's daughter by his first wife. But George's
admiration for the professor has been replaced by disillusionment. The play opens on the neighbouring estate of the wealthy
Zheltukhin and his sister Julia, who are being visited by the Sere-
bryakovs and the Voynitskys, and by Khrushchev (known as 'the
wood demon'), a passionate ecologist, medical practitioner, and
wealthy landowner. Zheltukhin has romantic feelings for Sonya,
Fyodr is a boor, George is both jealous and contemptuous of
Serebryakov, and Yelena is a beautiful but boringly high-minded
cold fish: there is a pervasive sense of mutual dislike at best,
loathing at worst, among this indolent group. The second act is
set in the dining room of the Serebryakov's house in the early
hours of the morning, during a thunderstorm. Khrushchev, sent
for to attend to Serebryakov, declares his love to Sonya, rather to
her embarrassment. The third act takes place in the Voynitsky
drawing room a fortnight later. The professor tells a family council
that he proposes to sell the estate. George is furious and, determin-
ed to do something to be remembered by, shoots himself offstage,
while Yelena in desperation asks Dyadin, a self-effacing neighbour,
to take her away. The last act is set outside Dyadin's house in a
forest clearing, two weeks after George's suicide. Khrushchev
arrives on some ecological mission, meeting the others on a picnic
outing. They bicker, are callous about George's death, and talk
of the need to serve humanity. As Yelena emerges from hiding to

be coolly received by her husband, the glow of a forest fire appears in the background, and Khrushchev hurries off, only to return for his horse when he discovers it is too far to walk. The others hide while Sonya declares her love to him, and they continue to observe as Fyodr proposes to Julia. The play ends with laughter, kisses, and general noise, while the woods continue to burn in the background.

[*The Wood Demon* is an interesting play in its own right, but, historically, has been mainly seen — and passed over — as an early draft of *Uncle Vanya*. Of the ten characters discussed in a letter from Chekhov to his intended collaborator, two disappear completely from Chekhov's single-handed version, and eight appear under different names, while four of the major characters reappear in *Uncle Vanya*. Of these, Chekhov's comments on Blagosvetlov (who becomes Serebryakov) and Korovin, who becomes Khrushchev in *The Wood Demon* and Astrov in *Uncle Vanya*, are most relevant.]

Alexander Platonych Blagosvetlov . . . comes from a priest's family and was educated at a church school. . . . He suffers from gout, rheumatism, insomnia, and noise in the ears. Acquired some landed property as part of his wife's dowry. Is impatient of mystics, visionaries, madmen, lyric poets, hypocrites; doesn't believe in God and is accustomed to looking at the world from a practical point of view. Business, deeds, action — and all the rest is just nonsense or plain foolery. —

Victor Petrovich Korovin — the Wood Demon — a landowner of between 30 and 33 years of age. A poet and landscape painter with a passionate feeling for nature. Once, when still at high school, he planted a silver birch tree in his own yard which, when it put out leaves and began to sway in the wind, to rustle and cast a tiny shadow, filled his heart with pride; he had helped God to create a new silver birch, had caused to exist one more birch tree on earth! This was the origin of his idiosyncratic creativity. He fulfils his ideas not on canvas, nor on paper, but in the earth; not in dead colour but with living organisms. . . . Forests serve the climate, climate affects character, and so on and so forth. There can be no civilization or happiness if the forests crash down before the axe, if the climate is cruel and harsh and if people are the same. . . . The future is terrible!

Chekhov, letter to A.S. Suvorin, 18 Oct. 1888

The play has turned out boring, mosaic-like, but nevertheless gives an impression of having been worked at. Some of my characters are positively new and there isn't a lackey in the entire play, nor a single comic character introduced for its own sake, nor the teeniest widow. There are eight characters all told and only three minor roles. Generally speaking I've tried to avoid everything superfluous and I think I've succeeded in this.

Chekhov, letter to Suvorin, 14 May 1889

In the play I portray a disgusting, selfish provincial fellow who for twenty years has been reading works on art but understands nothing about the subject – a man who brings despondency and gloom to all those near him, who is not accessible to laughter and music – and who, despite all this, is undoubtedly happy.

Chekhov, letter to Suvorin, 17 Oct. 1889

The Seagull

Comedy in four acts.
Written: 1896.
First production: Alexandrinsky Th., St. Petersburg, 17 Oct. 1896 (dir. E.P. Karpov; with Vera Komissarzhevskaya as Nina).
Revived: Moscow Art Th., 17 Oct. 1898 (dir. K.S. Stanislavsky and V.I. Nemirovich-Danchenko; with V.E. Meyerhold as Konstantin, O.L. Knipper as Arkadina, and Stanislavsky as Trigorin); Kammerspiele, Munich, 21 May 1911 (dir. Eugen Robert); Théâtre Comédie des Champs-Elysées, 25 Apr. 1922 (dir. Georges Pitoëff); Kamerny Th., Moscow, 20 July 1944 (dir. A. Tairov); Théâtre de l'Atelier, Apr. 1955 (dir. André Barsacq; des André Bakst); Royal Dramatic Th., Stockholm, 6 Jan. 1961 (dir. Ingmar Bergman).
First British production: Royalty Th., Glasgow, 2 Nov. 1909 (dir. George Calderon).
First London production: Little Th., 31 Mar. 1912 (dir. Maurice Elvey).
Revived: Little Th., 19 Oct. 1925 (dir. Esme Filmer; with Valerie Taylor as Nina and John Gielgud as Konstantin); Fortune Th., 25 Sept. 1929 (dir. Esme Filmer); New Th., 20 May 1936 (dir. Fyodr Komissarzhevsky; with Edith Evans as Arkadina, John Gielgud as Trigorin, and Peggy Ashcroft as Nina); Lyric Th., Hammersmith, 4 Oct. 1949 (dir. Irene Hentschel; with Paul Scofield as Konstantin and Mai Zetterling as Nina); Saville

Th., 2 Aug. 1956 (dir. Michael MacOwan); Old Vic, 1 Sept.
1960 (dir. John Fernald; with Tom Courtenay as Konstantin);
Queen's Th., 12 Mar. 1964 (dir. Tony Richardson; des. Jocelyn
Herbert; with Peggy Ashcroft as Arkadina, Vanessa Redgrave
as Nina, and Peter Finch as Trigorin); Aldwych Th., 25 May
1970 (Moscow Art Th. prod., dir. Boris Livanov); Greenwich
Th., 31 Jan. 1974 (dir. Jonathan Miller; with Irene Worth as
Arkadina and Robert Stephens as Trigorin); Lyric Th., 28 Oct.
1975 (dir. Lindsay Anderson; with Helen Mirren as Nina);
Royal Court Th., 8 Apr. 1981 (dir. Max Stafford-Clark).

First New York production: in Russian, St. Petersburg Dramatic
Co., 22 Dec. 1905 (dir. Paul Orlenev and Alla Nazimova).

Revived: Bandbox Th., 22 May 1916 (des. Lee Simonson);
Comedy Th., 9 Apr. 1929 (dir. Leo Bulgakov); 14th St. Th.,
16 Sept. 1929 (dir. Eve le Gallienne); Shubert Th., 28 Mar.
1938 (dir. Robert Milton; with Lynne Fontanne as Arkadina,
Alfred Lunt as Trigorin, and Margaret Webster as Masha);
Phoenix Th., 11 May 1954 (dir. Norris Houghton); 4th St. Th.,
22 Oct. 1956 (dir. David Ross); National Repertory Co., 5 Apr.
1964 (dir. Eve le Gallienne); Manhatten Th. Club, 30 Jan. 1975
(dir. Joseph Chaikin).

First published: Russian Idea, No. 12 (1896).

Translations: in *Two Plays by Tchekof,* trans. George Calderon
(London, 1912); in *Plays by Anton Tchekoff,* trans. Marian
Fell (New York, 1912); trans. Julius West (London, 1915); in
Plays from the Russian, Vol. I, trans. Constance Garnett
(London, 1923); trans. Stark Young (New York, 1938); in
Anton Chekhov: Plays and Stories, trans. S.S. Koteliansky
(London, 1967); in *Anton Chekhov: Plays,* trans. Elisaveta
Fen (Harmondsworth, 1959); in *Six Plays by Chekhov,* versions
by R.W. Corrigan (New York, 1962); in *Chekhov: the Major
Plays,* trans. Ann Dunnigan (New York, 1964); in *Anton
Chekhov: Four Plays,* trans. David Magarshack (New York,
1969); in *Oxford Chekhov II*; in *Anton Chekhov's Plays,*
trans. E.K. Bristow (New York, 1977); trans. Thomas Kilroy
(London, 1981). See also *The Seagull Produced by Stansilav-
sky: Production Score for the Moscow Art Theatre by K.S.
Stanislavsky,* ed. S.D. Balukhaty, trans. David Magarshack
(London, 1952).

*Peter Sorin is the brother of an egotistical actress, whose stage
name is Arkadina. Other inhabitants of his estate include her
son, Konstantin, an avant-garde writer with a mother-fixation;*

Arkadina's lover, Trigorin, a writer of 'realistic' fiction; Dr. Dorn, a stable family friend beloved by the estate manager's wife, Polina; a local schoolmaster, Medvedenko, who is in love with Polina's daughter Masha, who in turn is in love with Konstantin, who in his turn is in love with Nina Zarechnaya, the daughter of a wealthy neighbouring landowner. During the course of the play Nina falls in love with and is seduced by Trigorin, before being abandoned by him. Konstantin has written a 'symbolist' drama, in which Nina is to be solo performer in an outdoor setting. This play-within-the-play prompts derisory comments from Arkadina, and Konstantin, in petulant fury, brings the performance to a premature close. In the second act, Konstantin has shot a seagull, which he lays at Nina's feet and predicts his own suicide. Trigorin describes to Nina his compulsion to write in terms which do not accord with her romantic view: he notes the dead seagull and jots down a few notes for a short story in which someone like Nina will feature. By the third act, a week later, Konstantin has made a failed attempt at suicide and, during an intimate scene with his mother, squabbles with her. Nina has decided to leave and go on the stage, and agrees to meet Trigorin in Moscow. The fourth act begins two years later on a stormy autumn evening. Sorin has been taken ill, Arkadina and Trigorin are returning to the estate, and there is news that Nina is staying in the locality. Konstantin ruminates on his failure as a writer, and a semi-delirious, storm-soaked Nina enters from the veranda. She talks of her career as an actress and identifies herself, once again, with 'a seagull', while speaking of the need to 'bear her cross'. With her departure, Konstantin tears up all his manuscripts before he, too, leaves the stage. The others enter from dinner and a bang is heard offstage. Dorn exits, and returns to take Trigorin aside and inform him that 'Konstantin has shot himself'.

Can you imagine, I'm writing a play which I'll probably not complete before the end of November. I'm writing it not without pleasure, although I offend dreadfully against stage conventions. It's a comedy with three female and six male roles, four acts, a landscape (view of a lake) lots of talk about literature, little action and 180 lbs. of love.

Chekhov, letter to A.S. Suvorin, 21 Oct. 1895

I saw *The Seagull* without decor; I can't judge the play with
equanimity as the Seagull herself acted appallingly, blubbering
aloud all the time and Trigorin (the belle-lettrist) walked about
the stage and spoke like a paralytic; he has 'no will of his own'
which was interpreted by the actor in such a fashion that it made
me sick to look at it. However, it wasn't bad on the whole, quite
gripping. There were places where I even couldn't believe that I'd
written it myself.

Chekhov, letter to Maxim Gorky, 9 May, 1899

At the special performance he seemed to be trying to avoid me. I
waited for him in my dressing-room but he did not come. That
was a bad sign. I went to him myself. 'Scold me, Anton Pavlovich',
I begged him. 'Wonderful! Listen, it was wonderful! Only you
need torn shoes and checked trousers.' He would tell us no more.
What did it mean? Did he not wish to express his opinion? Was it
a jest to get rid of me? Was he laughing at me? Trigorin in *The
Seagull* was a young writer, a favourite of the women — and
suddenly he was to wear torn shoes and checked trousers! I
played the part in the most elegant of costumes — white trousers,
white waistcoat, white hat, and a handsome make-up.
  A year or more passed. Again I played the part of Trigorin in
The Seagull — and during one of the performances I suddenly
understood what Chekhov had meant. Of course the shoes must
be worn and the trousers checked and Trigorin must not be
handsome. In this lies the salt of the part: for young, inexperienced
girls it is important that a man should be a writer and print
touching and sentimental romances and the Nina Zarechnayas,
one after the other, will throw themselves on his neck, without
noticing that he is not handsome, that he wears checked trousers
or torn shoes.

Constantin Stanislavski, *My Life In Art*, trans. J.J. Robbins,
(Harmondsworth, 1967), p.335-6

I was rehearsing Trigorin in *The Seagull*. And of all things Anton
Pavlovich himself invites me to discuss the role with him. I go
along with some trepidation.
  'You know', Anton Pavlovich began, 'the fishing rods should
be sort of bent, home-made ones. He's made them himself with a
penknife. Your cigar's a good one. Maybe it shouldn't be such a
good one, but needs to be wrapped in silver paper.' Then he fell
silent, thought for a bit and said: 'But the important thing is the

fishing rods.' . . .

V.I. Kachalov, *Reminiscences,* cited in E.D. Surkov,
Chekhov i Teatr (Moscow, 1961), p.349

On the second occasion (11 September 1898) that Chekhov
attended rehearsals of *The Seagull* at the Moscow Art Theatre,
one of the actors told him that offstage there would be frogs
croaking, dragon-flies humming, and dogs barking.

'Why?' asked Anton Pavlovich in a dissatisfied tone. 'Because
it's realistic' − replied the actor. 'Realistic!' − repeated Chekhov
with a laugh. Then after a short pause he said: 'The stage is art.
There's a genre painting by Kramskoy in which the faces are
portrayed superbly. What would happen if you cut the nose out
of one of the paintings and substituted a real one? The nose
would be 'realistic' but the picture would be ruined.'

Cited in *Meyerhold on Theatre*, trans. and ed. Edward Braun
(London, 1969)

In the Adelphi Society's production neither Miss Kingston
[Arkadina] nor the Princess Bariatinsky [Nina] seemed to realize
that her individual part was important only in correlation with
the rest. It was not possible to be angry with Miss Kingston, for
the whole tradition of British acting . . . was against her in this
particular venture. But there was no sort of excuse of the Princess
Bariatinsky. . . . They had read their parts with care; they played
with energy and skill; individually they were not seriously wrong
for more than half the time; and they heavily impressed the
audience. In spite of all this − or, rather, because of it − they
succeeded in completely upsetting the balance and rhythm of the
play. So far as Chekhov's play was concerned my sensations were
exactly what they would have been if I saw the two legs of a man
I respected suddenly walking in different directions.

John Palmer, *Saturday Review,* CXIII (Apr. 1912)

Miss Miriam Lewes gave a really remarkable performance as the
middle-aged actress, Madam Treplev: both the woman, selfish,
emotional, disappointed, and the actress, the least degree flashy
in her bearing and histrionic in her demonstrations, were perfectly
represented. Miss Valerie Taylor had no easy part with Nina, as
unmitigatedly serious as the stage Tess, but she spoke charmingly,
looked very appealing, and was very pathetic in her last big scene.

Mr. Randolph McLeod as Trigorin, the famous man of letters, looked (to my thinking) at once too young and too dashing: surely Chekhov did not want a Latin Quarter *panache* in this celebrated author in whom is illustrated the spell that mere artistic fame exercises. Trigorin should have been uglier, older, shabbier, and, I think, harder. . . .

Mr. John Gielgud's Konstantin . . . acted fluently and intelligently, but his manner of speech was really most unsuitable to the part. This is not an easy sort of thing to talk about, and I don't suggest a cultivated affectation of speech. But he has a kind of prunes-and-prisms mode of speaking, with 'her' pronounced roughly as 'heh', and 'mother' as 'metheh', which might go excellently with a drawing-room comedy sort of a part, but gives an air of unreality to his performance when one sees him in alien or archaic garb, or as a 'hero'.

J.C. Squire, London Mercury, XIII (Dec. 1925)

What is the secret of Chekhov? I remember poor Basil Macdonald Hastings coming up to me, immediately after the first act of *The Cherry Orchard* at Hammersmith, and saying, 'Lenin was right'. He had just been watching a crowd of dreary Russians, all bemoaning their fate, all talking about their woes, all worrying over nothing, yet all in trouble of their own making. Then he suddenly realized, I suppose, that a revolution of some sort was necessary to stop that kind of thing.

I went through the same sort of feeling for two acts of *The Seagull*, in which, immediately the curtain rose, a man asked a young woman, 'Why are you dressed in black?' and she replied, 'I am in mourning for my life because it is so sad.' It sounded like the beginning of a funeral. Then, one after another, all the other characters came on, and moaned and mooned. . . . Then, somehow, the play began to get hold of me. . . .

Chekhov is all shadows, all despair. I never saw a moral in it, nor any ennobling thought. It is merely the ineffectiveness of the effete, put down for analysis. Yet there is nothing to analyze except the effect upon yourself. You listen, not to the sound of the words, but to the beating of your own heart in sympathy. 'Yet', you reflect, 'there are thousands of people as sorely stricken as these in every town in England. Are they inarticulate, or do they only express themselves when you are not there?' I expect they just get on with their jobs.

Hannen Swaffer, Sunday Express, 29 Sept. 1929

In *Myself and the Theatre* M. Komisarjevsky has written: 'Chekhov made quite clear, during rehearsals of *The Seagull*, what actors should not do when acting his plays. "They're acting too much', he would say. "I wish they would act less. Why walk in such an obvious way? That fellow doesn't look a bit like a novelist. He's simply a leading actor, not a novelist. Masha is over-acting: my Masha is simplicity itself. Everything must be done as artlessly as possible.'

It is odd, then, that so much of this should be applicable to the present production of *The Seagull* at the New Theatre. The play is, and should be, almost unbearably moving, and you should not be able to see it without feeling rocked and shaken to your own foundations. But somehow it is all a little too carefully, too elaborately done, beautifully, but too beautifully. There is no waywardness, no rawness, nothing that is not competent and controlled. And, frankly, too many of the parts are too badly miscast. Mr. John Gielgud is too bloodless as the novelist, Miss Martita Hunt too showy as the dismal Masha. Miss Edith Evans, as the famous actress, glitters too brightly to evoke compassion. Most of all, Miss Peggy Ashcroft, as Nina, the stage-struck girl, acts too well and too competently. . . . For instance, she cries beautifully in the last act, but Nina's tears are not beautiful; they should be dreadful paroxysms of sobbing.

J.G.B., *Evening News*, 21 May 1936

The settings . . . were heavy and unimaginative, suppressing the beauty of the moonlit lake: there was no toss and glitter of production to galvanize us into enchantment, though Irene Hentschel's production had a certain slow grace and understanding. But a performance of careful thought and beautiful, unhurried sensitivity by the young actor Paul Scofield as Constantin, caught at the heartstrings; and although Mai Zetterling as Nina was hampered by a Swedish accent, and failed sufficiently to grow in anguish and experience in the last act, her child-like delicacy of perception gave a moving radiance to the earlier scenes and her suffering was never in doubt.

Audrey Williamson, *Theatre of Two Decades* (London 1951), p.206

The opening of *The Seagull* at the Queen's Theatre . . . was a personal triumph for Redgrave, who decisively implanted the figure of Nina as the play's emotional centre. . . . Devine appeared as Dorn, which for many people was the finest performance of his career. Gielgud, with his long memory of the spotty boy who played Mercutio for the OUDS, pronounced it, 'amazing. He looked more handsome than I'd ever seen him in my life. Divinely sexy and attractive.' Strolling on in his panama hat, and observing the passionate follies of his companions with the detachment of one whose appetites have been satisfied, he was indeed the image of a successful lady-killer in retirement. But the performance was also free from the usual accompanying cynicism. He played Dorn as a man who knows all about human egoism, and tries to do what little good he can in a generally hopeless situation: accepting Nina's gift of flowers with sincere chivalry, and submitting without protest when the jealous Polina snatches them away. 'How hysterical they are! . . . And what a lot of love . . . But what can I do, my child? What?' As Devine played that line, Dorn really wanted to know.

Irving Wardle, *The Theatres of George Devine* (London, 1978), p.258

With the best of intentions it is hard for an American — it is absurd for him to try — to take seriously the neurasthenic maunderings which in this play are paraded in the guise of dramatic complications. . . . The only answer that a normal American can make to this sort of thing is that, if the boy [Konstantin] had had the advantage of some athletic sport, he would doubtless have worked off most of the vague feelings which he mistook for the stirrings of genius.

H. de W. Fuller, *The Nation*, 1 June 1916

The production as a whole, whatever shortcomings it may have had, was never false. However short it may have come of that necessary utmost penetration and that mutual current among all the characters, it moved always with honesty, and with respect for the work of art in hand, and without specious and stagey yearnings. . . . Miss Le Gallienne herself played Masha with sincerity and with an admirable scaling of her role to its due place in the play. The prime limitation of her acting is that it still lacks the right degree of movement from the centre outward. You can see this even in a single simple gesture toward another person in the scene, you can see that the gesture, or movement, does not proceed enough from the nerves, emotion, idea, from which it first arises; it is an indication rather than acting. Miss Merle

43

Maddern, a newcomer among these players, in the brilliant role of Madame Treplev, the actress, is for the more obvious actress-moments very good; in the richer and more complex depths of the character, she only grazes its quality.

Stark Young, *The New Republic*, 9 Oct. 1929

As Mme. Trepleff, the vain, selfish actress, Miss Fontanne cheapens the part considerably by overacting and gaudily wigging it. As Trigorin, Mr. Lunt has the invaluable gift of making his lines sound as though he had just invented them on the spur of the moment. But he, too, seems a little obtuse to the spiritual solitude of the play as a whole. . . . As Nina, the sensitive country maiden who flings herself at a celebrity, Uta Hagen is grace and aspiration incarnate. Richard Whorf's Constantine, the young writer, gives a sensible, original performance up to his last scene when his suffering becomes grotesque. As the venerable counsellor, Sydney Greenstreet acts as well as he can in a performance that does not give him time enough to ruminate like a disappointed man. . . . In fact, Margaret Webster is the only member of the cast who plays with perception of the evanescent life that is hovering under and around the written skeleton of the drama. As Masha, the love-sick one, the melancholy tippler, her acting is rich and aware. . . . But only half of the play is to be found on the stage of the Shubert just now. It is the literal half. The other half is the genius of Chekhov's *The Seagull*.

Brooks Atkinson, *New York Times*, 29 Mar. 1938

Uncle Vanya

'Scenes from country life in four acts.'
*Written: c.*1897
First production: at provincial theatres in Odessa, Kiev, Saratov, Tbilisi, 1897; Moscow Art Th., 26 Oct. 1899 (dir. K.S. Stanislavsky and V.I. Nemirovich-Danchenko; with Stanislavsky as Astrov and Olga Knipper as Yelena).
Revived: National Th., Prague, 20 Apr. 1901 (dir. Josef Smaha); Berliner Th., Berlin, 1904 (dir. Ernst Belisch); Théâtre du Vieux-Colombier, 15 Apr. 1921 (dir. Georges Pitoëff); Mark Taper Forum, Los Angeles, 13 Aug. 1969 (dir. Harold Clurman); Den Nationale Scene, Bergen, 1971 (dir. Otto Homlung); Kammerspiele, Munich, 28 Aug. 1972 (dir. Erwin Axer).
First London production: Aldwych Th., 11 May 1914 (dir. Guy

Rathbone).

Revived: Royal Court Th., 27 Nov. 1921 (dir. Fyodr Komissarz-
hevski; with Leon Quartermaine as Astrov); Barnes Th. 16
Feb. 1926 (dir. Fyodr Komissarzhevski; with Robert
Farquharson as Vanya and Jean Forbes-Robertson as Sonya);
Westminster Th., 5 Feb. 1937 (dir. Michael Macowan; (with
Harcourt Williams as Vanya); Westminster Th., 2 Sept. 1943
(dir. Normal Marshall; with Frith Banbury as Astrov); New
Th., 16 Jan. 1945 (dir. John Burrell; des. Tanya Moiseiwitsch;
with Ralph Richardson as Vanya, Laurence Olivier as Astrov,
and Sybil Thorndike as Marina); Sadlers Wells Th., 20 May
1958 (Moscow Art Th., dir. M. Kedrov); Old Vic. Th., 19 Nov.
1963 (dir. Laurence Olivier; des. Sean Kenny; with Michael
Redgrave as Vanya, Olivier as Astrov, Max Adrian as Serebryakov, and Sybil Thorndike as Marina); Royal Court Th.,
24 Feb. 1970 (dir. Anthony Page; with Paul Scofield as Vanya,
and Colin Blakely as Astrov); National Th., 18 May 1982
(dir. Michael Bogdanov; des. John Bury; with Michael Bryant
as Vanya).

First New York production: in Russian, by Moscow Art Th.,
Jolson's 59th St. Th., 28 Jan. 1924.

Revived: Morosco Th., 24 May 1929 (dir. Harold Winston);
Cort Th., 15 Apr. 1930 (dir. Jed Harris); Fourth St. Th.,
31 Jan. 1956 (dir. David Ross); Circle-in-the-Square/Joseph
E. Levine Th., 4 June 1973 (dir. Mike Nichols).

First published: 1897.

Translations: in *Plays by Anton Tchekoff*, trans. Marian Fell
(New York, 1912); trans. F.A. Saphro (Boston, 1922); in
The Moscow Art Theatre Series of Russian Plays, ed. Oliver M.
Sayler, trans. Jennie Covan (New York, 1922); in *Plays from
the Russian, Vol. 1,* trans. Constance Garnett (London, 1923);
trans. Rose Caylor (New York, 1930); in *Five Famous Plays
by Anton Tchekoff*, trans. Julius West and Marian Fell
(London, 1939); trans. Stark Young (New York, 1956); in
Anton Chekhov: Plays, trans. Elisaveta Fen (Harmondsworth,
1959); in *The Storm and Other Russian Plays*, trans. David
Magarshack (London, 1960); in *Oxford Chekhov III*; in
Chekhov: the Major Plays, trans. Ann Dunnigan (New York,
1964); in *Anton Chekhov's Plays*, trans. E.K. Bristow (New
York, 1977); trans. Pam Gems (London, 1979).

---

*The play is set on the country estate owned by Professor Serebry-
akov's daughter, Sonya, to which he has retired in company with*

*his 27-year-old second wife, Yelena. For the past 25 years the
estate has been managed by Sonya, with his first wife's brother,
Ivan Voynitsky (Uncle Vanya), but Vanya's former respect for
the professor is quickly replaced by disillusionment. He becomes
enamoured of the professor's young wife, as does a local landowner and doctor, Astrov, who neglects his other duties. Sonya is
secretly in love with him and admires his ecological enthusiasms.
The play opens in the garden on a sultry afternoon, and the
breaking storm accompanies the action of the second act, during
which Astrov tends Serebryakov's rheumatism. There follows a
moment of reconciliation, after the storm, between Sonya and
Yelena, in which the one confesses her love for Astrov, the other
her admiration of him. At the beginning of the third act, Yelena
seeks an opportunity to sound Astrov out about his feelings for
Sonya: he misinterprets her questioning, and she is both repelled
and attracted by his description of her as 'vampire' and 'furry
weasel'. Serebryakov then announces to the family that he proposes to sell the estate. Vanya protests and accuses the professor
of ruining his life. As Serebryakov attempts an offstage reconciliation with him, a shot is heard and the professor reappears pursued
by Vanya who fires a second time before sinking on a chair in
exhausted frustration. At the beginning of the last act Serebryakov and Yelena have announced their departure. Vanya cannot
forgive himself for having missed the professor twice, but Serebryakov tells him to forgive and forget and they embrace as if nothing
had happened. Astrov, who has managed a brief embrace with
Yelena, announces 'Finita la comedia!' and that he, too, is leaving.
Vanya returns to his accounts while Sonya embarks on her speech
which concludes the play stressing that life goes on and that,
finally, they will find peace and rest.*

In response to your instruction I hasten to answer your letter in
which you ask about the final scene between Yelena and Astrov.
You write that Astrov behaves towards Yelena in this scene like
the most passionate lover 'clutching at feeling like a drowning
man at a straw'. But this is absolutely and totally wrong! Astrov
loves Yelena, she captivates him with her beauty, but in the last
act he already knows that nothing will come of this, that Yelena
is disappearing for ever as far as he is concerned – and he talks to
her in this scene in the same tone as he speaks of the heat in

Africa, and kisses her quite simply for want of anything better to do. If Astrov conducts this scene in a violent fashion then the whole quiet and listless mood of Act 4 will be lost.

Chekhov, letter to Olga Knipper, 20 Sept. 1899

Is Yelena Andreyevna, the professor's wife, an average intelligent woman, who is a thinking and decent person, or is she an apathetic idle woman, incapable of thinking or even loving? I cannot reconcile myself to this second interpretation and I dare to hope that my understanding of her as a reasoning, thinking person who is made unhappy by her dissatisfaction with her present life is the correct one.

From a letter from an amateur performer,
Marianna Pobedinskaya, to Chekhov, 30 Jan. 1903

Your opinion of Yelena Andreyevna is completely justified. . . . Yelena Andreyevna may produce the impression of being incapable of thinking or even loving, but while I was writing *Uncle Vanya* I had something completely different in mind.

Chekhov, letter replying to Pobedinskaya, 5 Feb. 1903

Chekhov would hint to us of an interesting thought or some characteristic trait of his creations. For instance, we talked of the role of Uncle Vanya himself. It is accepted that Uncle Vanya is a member of the landed gentry who manages the estate of the old Professor Serebriakov. It would seem that we had not far to look. The costume and the general appearance of a landed gentleman are known to all, high boots, a cap, sometimes a horse-whip, for it is taken for granted that he rides horseback a great deal. It was so that we painted him to ourselves. But Chekhov was terribly indignant.

'Listen', he said in great excitement, 'everything is said there. You didn't read the play.' We looked in to the original, but we found no hint there unless we were to reckon several words about a silk tie which Uncle Vanya wore.

'Here it is, here it is written down,' Chekhov tried to persuade us. 'What is written down?' We were in amazement. 'A silk tie?'

'Of course. Listen, he has a wonderful tie; he is an elegant, cultured man. It is not true that our landed gentry walk about in boots smeared with tar. They are wonderful people. They dress well. They order their clothes in Paris. It is all written down.' . . .

The night of the first performance arrived.... In the intermissions [Chekhov] would come into my dressing-room and praise me, and at the end he made only one remark about the scene where Astrov goes away.

'He whistles. Listen, he whistles! Uncle Vanya is crying, but Astrov whistles!' Again, I could not get any more out of him. But, knowing the laconical nature of his remarks and their deep meaning, I broke my head in thought over the new problems he had placed before me.

'How is that?' I said to myself. 'Sadness, hopelessness, and merry whistling?' But his remark came to life of itself during one of the later performances. Believing in what Chekhov said, I whistled. What was going to happen? I felt at once that the whistle was truthful, that Astrov must whistle.

Constantin Stanislavsky, *My Life in Art,* p.338-42

Anton Pavlovich once saw a performance of *Uncle Vanya.* In the third act Sonya went down on her knees on the line 'Father, you must be merciful!', and kissed his hands. 'You mustn't do that, that isn't what drama is', said Anton Pavlovich. 'The whole meaning or drama of a person lies internally, not in outer manifestations. There was drama in Sonya's life prior to this moment, and there will be subsequently, but this is just an occurrence, a continuation of the pistol shot. And the pistol shot is not a drama either, but an occurrence.

I.S. Butova, *Reminiscences,* quoted in E.D. Surkov, *Chekhov i Teatr* (Moscow, 1961), p.346

As a gallery of futile and worrying personages, *Uncle Vanya* may have its value; as a stage play it is a desolate, dreary, competent piece of work, no doubt good for us to see once, but not, we trust, a second time. Alas, that so much labour should be devoted by the author and actors to so distressing a picture of the vacuity and bitterness of life!

Egan Mew, *The Academy*, 23 May 1914, p.662-3

Uncle Vanya is an unforgettably good play.... Have you not felt that fog in your throat on English lawns, in English houses? Indeed, the main point of difference between this spell-bound cultivated Russian society and the English variety is not in our favour. If Chekhov's intellectuals are half-dead, the other half of them is very much, painfully much, alive. They suffer more consciously; there is intensity in their lassitude; at least they torture themselves, and each other, by displaying each his own bankruptcy. They are not comatose and outwardly contented, but sensitive, self-conscious, and critical.

Desmond MacCarthy, *New Statesman,* 16 May 1914

Uncle Vanya is a play not far removed in construction from the old time melodrama thrillers of the American stage. After long detours of what is presumed to be flowery dialogue and graceful gesture, intense, impassioned climaxes are reached, and the audience last night ... appeared to recognize these warmer moments and to appreciate them. ... The performance of the doctor by Constantin Stanislavsky is easily one of the most appealing which the director of the Moscow Players has given, and Alla Tarasova as Sonya, the love-stricken girl, is natural and fine in her part. Indeed, there is a smoothness throughout such as has marked all the performances of the company.

The World, New York, 29 Jan. 1924

Directed ably, with a sort of intellectual understanding, by Harold Winston, the performance conveys the last two acts splendidly. Morris Carnovsky, in a make-up that unhappily suggests Shylock, is an actor to be reckoned with as Uncle Vanya — strong, brooding, clear-cut. As Sonya, Rose Keane acts with life and beauty the most attractive part in the play. Ara Gerald, as the stepmother, is firm and direct; and Hubert Druce, as the windy professor, is delightfully overbearing. Cast in a part beyond his years, Franchot Tone portrays a doctor who lacks the stability the part suggests. *Uncle Vanya* is not one of the finest Chekhov plays, either in the scope of the story or the construction, nor is the performance uniformly ideal. But it is genuine. Occasionally its random observations leap out of the action like rifle shots, accurate, unerring.

Brooks Atkinson, *New York Times*, 25 May 1929

What distinguishes Mr. Harris's production from other versions of Chekhov that have been seen here is simply the variety and the greater vitality that he has induced from the endless succession of hints and subtleties. It has the solidity of Chekhov's realism, and that realism is, of course, irrefutable; likewise it has the scintillant

49

and more inaccessible flashes that make the Chekhov plays comedies in a wide, sardonic sense. Despair pervades *Uncle Vanya*, but compassion illuminates it; and under Mr. Harris's direction those searching elements play against each other pulsingly. . . . Mr. Osgood Perkins's Michael Astroff is vigorous, tensely responsive, quietly bitter; Walter Connolly's performance as Uncle Vanya represents a torrential and passionate outbreak of cumulative hatred. . . . Lillian Gish, who returns to the stage after many years in the motion pictures, curiously brings to the role of Helena the best virtues of the silent cinema style − an assured case of movement and a telling pantomime. . . .

John Hutchens, *Theatre Arts Monthly,* Apr. 1930

Nothing could be more difficult for a dramatist than this creation of a young woman who has married an old man, truly in love with the glamour of his fame and the hint of the ideal that lay in him, and who now, asking of life only peace, is drawn toward, and at the same time flees, its passionate desires. The woman Miss Gish presents is as successfully created as Chekhov's. That frail figure and delicate, honest spirit are unforgettable, and the line and movement in their grace and perfect timing are unforgettable.

Stark Young, *New Republic*, 30 Apr. 1930, p.299-300

Vanya makes two attempts to shoot the old Professor, and misses. The English tendency is to treat the attempt and the wild quarrel that precedes it as extravagant farce, for the plain reason that only in farces do Englishmen so wildly express their feelings as these Russians do in this scene. Again, in the opening of the next act, Vanya, looking out of the ruins of his life and in a mood of demented despair, speaks abruptly of the shame of having missed − of having missed twice; and the English tendency is to receive the remark as if it were the cry of an old gentleman who remembered that, years ago, he dropped two catches against Harrow at Lord's.

To lay too much emphasis on this distortion would be a mistake. A keen and intelligent audience knows its Chekhov too well nowadays to guffaw in the wrong place. But the distorting tendency remains and makes it almost impossible for producer and actors, who are bound to play to their audience, to communicate the truth of Chekhov's mingling of comedy with tragedy, which happens to be a compound, not a mixture. They are, as it were, forced to lay emphasis on lines that will produce a laugh, whereas

Chekhov though he wrote often for laughter — sometimes outright and sometimes coolly ironic — treated his work as a fluid whole and did not deliberately write what, in the technical jargon of our theatre, is called 'lines'.

This is the difficulty by which the present production is affected. One sees it at every point . . . But the effect of what may be called 'audience distortion' on Vanya and the Doctor is remarkable. Mr. Harcourt Williams's Vanya, though it has a cloudy opening, becomes as it advances a very distinguished portrait, but it is again and again coarsened . . . by the audience's tendency to give a peculiarly English twist to the words. Mr. Cecil Trouncer, as the Doctor, suffers greater damage because, instead of resisting the English twist, he welcomes and uses it to get laughs.

The Times, 6 Feb. 1937

Mr. Burrell has a fine company. He handles it sensitively and they respond beautifully, demonstrating that Chekhov can use as much acting genius as he can get. Dame Sybil Thorndike is by no means wasted in the tiny part of the old nurse whose elderly, brooding eyes reflect the disturbing effects of gout and beauty on her children with a calm appreciation which sometimes sharpens and sometimes softens an outline. The exasperated forcible-feeble Vanya of Mr. Ralph Richardson is the perfect compound of absurdity and pathos; and Mr. Laurence Olivier's Astrov becomes, as it advances, a very distinguished portrait, in which superficial weakness and underlying strength are brought out in their proper proportions. Poor little Sonya, who fails to be loved or even noticed by the man she loves, but at least fails nobly, is played by Miss Joyce Redman with a kind of stilled sincerity that demands an equal response of the heart and of the mind. And Miss Margaret Leighton's Yelena is entirely satisfying in its lazy, graceful and watchful poise.

The Times, 17 Jan. 1945

Individually each star was gleaming, but there was a mist over the whole which dimmed the production and made it seem far away. Mr. Olivier would give us a magnificent ten minutes of the Doctor and then we could almost hear him say: 'Passed to you, Ralph'. Whereupon Mr. Richardson would give us a splendid ten minutes of Uncle Vanya. Miss Thorndike was so convincing as the old nurse that she almost raised the Samovar to a principal part, Miss Leighton enchanted the ear and delighted the eye but never convinced us for a moment that she had really married the old Professor. On the other hand, George Ralph was so good as the impoverished landowner that he appeared to be playing Chekhov while the others were from a different author altogether. Little Miss Joyce Redman did her best with the plain daughter, but I suggest that she failed to grasp the meaning of that pitiful scene at the end, when, robbed of her Doctor and all hope of life, she comforts poor Vanya with heartbroken assurances that now they will have rest and peace and eventually find happiness.

Beverley Baxter, *Evening Standard*, 29 Jan. 1945

There is a tide in the affairs of men; and Chekhov's people have all missed it. When the moment comes, the chance of a new life, their attention is somehow distracted, and the old life claims them again: they meet each other always at the wrong time, too early, or too late, so that the splendid confrontation scenes beloved of other playwrights never take place. Yet they might have done so, if only life were better organized; and this 'if only', this constant nagging sense that things might have been otherwise, is what gives his plays their abiding power.

The eponymous anti-hero of *Uncle Vanya* discovers too late that the intellectual brother-in-law he has spent his best years supporting is a greedy old fraud; Astrov, the one-time idealist, falls in love with the fraud's pretty bride when he is too far sunk in self-disgust to be capable of love; and Sonya, the fraud's daughter, is too young for Astrov, who has long since betrayed the ideals for which she loves him. One is always aware of a discrepancy between what is and what might have been; and by a sort of cruel kindness, Chekhov forces his characters, in the end, to see each other as they really are.

Laurence Olivier's production . . . enshrines two superlative performances: his own as Astrov, a visionary maimed by self-knowledge and dwindled into a middle-aged *roué,* and Michael Redgrave's as Vanya, torn between self-assertion and self-deprecation, and taking the stage in a tottering, pigeon-toed stride that boldly amalgamates both.

Kenneth Tynan, *Tynan Right and Left* (London, 1967), p.110

The current Lyttelton revival, directed by Michael Bogdanov, cannot obliterate the memories of those summit performances by Olivier (Astrov) and Redgrave (Vanya) in 1963; and its interpretation over-simplifies some of the play's emotional complexities.

But it establishes its narrowing vision of Chekhov's world, as a whole, with a clarity, strength and consistency of acting, direction, and design that compel respect as well as disagreement. In some ways, indeed, this production surpasses its near-legendary predecessor. John Bury's set, for example, seems a more imaginative solution that Sean Kenny's of the design problems presented by these 'scenes from country life'. . . . It is authentically specific and evocative, suggesting both the inner and outer space of this 26-room house and its surrounding steppes and forests without smothering detail and excessive abstraction. . . . Cherie Lunghi's performance of Yelena, perhaps the most difficult role in *Uncle Vanya* and one which defeated Joan Greenwood in 1962, is a convincingly unflattering portrait . . . [although the] emphasis on Yelena as a shallow, selfish, idle, cold, and rather stupid young woman errs a bit on the ungenerous side. . . . Ms. Lunghi's performance reinforces one's impression that Mr. Bogdanov is seeking to deromanticize the characters. . . . Mr. Bryant's Vanya is not only much closer to the grave than Mr. Redgrave's (and Chekhov's): he is more capable and experienced, less wildly absurd, and far less poignant. . . . Patti Love has made [Sonya] so plain, gauche, ungainly, almost clownish that, whatever Astrov says, he would never for a moment, one feels, have considered her as a possible mistress or wife. . . . In keeping with this production's approach, Astrov's ecological idealism and medical altruism are somewhat muted, and his growing coarseness, booziness and, desperation are emphasized in a powerful magnetic performance by Dinsdale Landen.

Richard Findlater, *Plays and Players*, July 1982, p.24-5

Three Sisters

Drama in four acts.
Written: 1900–01.
First production: Moscow Art Th., 31 Jan. 1901 (dir. K.S.
    Stanislavsky and V.I. Nemirovich-Danchenko; with Stanislavsky
    as Vershinin, Olga Knipper as Masha, and V.E. Meyerhold as
    Tuzenbakh).
Revived: National Th., Prague, 1907; Volksbühne, Berlin, 1926
    (dir. Jürgen Fehling); Théâtre des Arts, Paris, 26 Jan. 1929
    (dir. Georges Pitoëff); Moscow Art Th., 20 Apr. 1940 (dir.
    V.I. Nemirovich-Danchenko); Staatstheater, Stuttgart, 1965
    (dir. Rudolf Noelte); Theatre Behind the Gate, Prague, 1967
    (dir. Otomar Krejca; des Josef Svoboda); Residenztheater,

Münich, 22 June 1978 (dir. Ingmar Bergman).
First London production: Royal Court Th., 8 Mar. 1920.
Revived: Barnes Th., 16 Feb. 1926 (dir. Fyodr Komissarzhevski;
  with John Gielgud as Tuzenbakh); Fortune Th., 23 Oct. 1929
  (dir. Fyodr Komissarzhevski); Old Vic Th., 12 Nov. 1935;
  Queen's Th., 28 Jan. 1938 (dir. Michel St. Denis; with Gwen
  Ffrangcon-Davies as Olga, Peggy Ashcroft as Irina, George
  Devine as Andrey, John Gielgud as Vershinin, and Michael
  Redgrave as Tuzenbakh); Sadlers Wells Th., 16 May 1958
  (Moscow Art Th., dir. Yosif Raevski); Aldwych Th., 3 May
  1965 (Actors' Studio Th., dir. Lee Strasberg); Royal Court
  Th., 18 Apr. 1967 (dir. William Gaskill; with Glenda Jackson
  as Masha and Alan Webb as Chebutykin); Old Vic Th., 4 July
  1967 (dir. Laurence Olivier; des. Josef Svododa; with Robert
  Stephens as Vershinin and Joan Plowright as Masha);
  Cambridge Th., 26 June 1976 (dir. Jonathan Miller; des.
  Patrick Robertson; with Janet Suzman as Masha); RSC at The
  Warehouse, 2 Apr. 1980 (dir. Trevor Nunn; des. John Napier).
First New York production: Jolson's 59th St. Th., 29 Jan. 1923
  (Moscow Art Th., production).
Revived: Clive Rep. Th., 26 Oct. 1926 (dir. Eve Le Gallienne);
  Longacre Th., Oct. 1939 (dir. Samuel Rosen); Ethel Barrymore
  Th., 21 Dec. 1942 (dir. Guthrie McClintick; with Katharine
  Cornell as Masha and Judith Anderson as Olga); 4th St.
  Theatre, 25 Feb. 1955 (dir. David Ross).
First published: in *Russian Idea,* No. 2 (1901).
Translations: in *Plays by Anton Tchekoff, Second Series,* trans.
  Julius West (New York, 1916); in *The Moscow Art Theatre
  Series of Russian Plays,* trans. Jennie Covan; in *Plays from
  the Russian, Vol. II,* trans. Constance Garnett (London,
  1923); trans. Stark Young (New York, 1941); in *A Treasury of
  Russian Literature,* trans. B.G. Guerney (London, 1948); in
  Anton Chekhov: Plays, trans. Elisaveta Fen (Harmondsworth,
  1959); in *Oxford Chekhov III*; in *Chekhov: the Major Plays,*
  trans. Ann Dunnigan (New York, 1964); in *Anton Chekhov:
  Four Plays,* trans. David Magarshack (New York, 1969); trans.
  Moura Budberg (London, 1971); in *Anton Chekhov's Plays,*
  trans. E.K. Bristow (New York, 1977); trans; Brian Friel
  (Dublin, 1981); trans. Michael Frayn (London, 1983).

*The action takes place in the house, situated in a remote garrison
town, owned by three sisters and their brother, which they have
inherited from their dead parents. The sisters have their hearts*

*set on returning to Moscow, where they spent their childhood,
resting their hopes upon their brother's obtaining a professorship
at Moscow University. The action of the play begins with the
arrival of Natasha, a local girl, who marries the brother, Andrei,
and gradually ousts the sisters from their home. The first act
celebrates the 'name-day' of the youngest sister, Irina, and the
arrival of the new battery commander Vershinin, who calls to pay
his respects. The second act opens about a year and a half later
during carnival week: Natasha and Andrei have married and have
a son Bobik, while Masha, the middle sister, bored with her schoolmaster husband, has struck up a relationship with the philandering
Vershinin, whose wife keeps threatening suicide. A solipsistic
junior officer, Solyony, declares his love for Irina and threatens
to kill any rival, the most obvious being an unattractive lieutenant
of self-consciously German origin, Baron Tuzenbakh. The third
act takes place against the background of a fire in the town: it
is a year or so later, and Natasha has a second child. A drunken
military doctor, Chebutykin, a permanent house guest, soliloquizes
morosely on his misanthropy and the nature of existence. Irina
has hysterics at rumours of the battery's departure, but agrees
to marry the baron so long as this means they will all go to
Moscow. By the last act it is early autumn, and the garrison is on
the move. Solyony has challenged the baron to a duel, which the
doctor has done nothing to prevent. The semi-hysteria of Masha's
farewell to Vershinin is interrupted by the sound of a pistol shot,
while a military band plays cheerfully. Chebutykin announces
that the baron has been killed. The three sisters gather together as
Olga, the eldest, responds to Chebutykin's assertion that 'Nothing
matters', with the refrain 'If only we knew, if only we knew!'*

Ivan Tchekhov, Anton's brother, was teacher in an elementary
school in Voskressensk, near Moscow, a small town resembling a
big village. The life there went on in the old way, living was very
cheap, and it was unspoiled by townspeople. Quartered in the
town was a battery whose chief was Colonel B.I. Mayevsky, an ener-
getic and social man. The well-known Slavophile V.D. Golokhvastov,
whose wife wrote dramas and comedies for the state-supported
theatres of Petersburg and Moscow, also lived there. Each year
the Tchekhov family used to come for their summer holidays to
Ivan and stay with him at the school. Ivan was tutor to Colonel

Mayevsky's children, and through him became friendly with the battery officers and with the Moscow intellectuals who used to spend the summer in Voskressensk. During their holidays the Tchekhovs made friends with these people, and when Anton got his medical degree in 1884 and went to Voskressensk, he soon made quite a wide circle of acquaintances. The centre of the local life was the Mayevsky family with their children Annie, Sonya, and Alioshka, with whom Anton became fast friends. . . . Here he got the knowledge of military life which he used in his play *The Three Sisters*.

> M.P. Chekhov, 'Tchekhov and His Subjects', in *The Life and Letters of Anton Tchekhov*, trans. S.S. Koteliansky and Philip Tomlinson (London, 1925)

Describe at least one rehearsal of *Three Sisters* to me. Isn't there anything which needs adding or subtracting? Are you acting well, my darling? But watch out now! Don't pull a sad face in the first act. Serious, yes, but not sad. People who have long carried a grief within themselves and have become accustomed to it only whistle and frequently withdraw into themselves. So you can often be thoughtfully withdrawn on stage during conversations. Do you see?

> Chekhov, letter to Olga Knipper, who played Masha, 2 Jan. 1901

Here are the answers to your questions: 1) Irina doesn't know that Tuzenbakh is going to a duel, but guesses that something untoward happened the previous evening which could have important and even unfortunate consequences. And when a woman intuits something, she always says 'I knew it, I knew it'. 2) Chebutykin just sings the words 'Be so good as to accept one of these dates'. They're words from an operetta which was once performed at the Hermitage. I don't remember the name of it. . . . Chebutykin mustn't sing anything else otherwise his exit will be too lengthy. 3) Solyony does actually think he's similar to Lermontov; but of course he's nothing of the sort — it's even laughable to think so. He should be made-up to look like Lermontov. There is a tremendous likeness but only in the opinion of Solyony.

> Chekhov, letter to I.A. Tikhomirov, who played Fedotik, 14 Jan. 1901

Of course everything must be quiet on stage in the third act so that a sense of people's exhaustion can be felt and the fact that they want to sleep. What's the point of all the noise? It's indicated in the text where the alarm bells are rung off-stage.

Chekhov, letter to Olga Knipper, 17 Jan. 1901

Well, how are the *Three Sisters*? Judging by your letters you're all talking complete nonsense. Why the noise in Act 3? Why? There's only distant noise, off-stage, a vague muffled noise, while everyone on stage is tired, almost falling asleep. If you spoil Act 3 then the whole play falls through and they'll hiss me at my time of life.

Chekhov, letter to Olga Knipper, 20 Jan. 1901

My darling girl, Masha's confession in Act 3 is not in the least confession-like, but only a frank conversation. Deliver it nervously, but not despairingly; don't shout, smile from time to time, but most importantly deliver it so as to convey a sense of the night's fatigue. Also to convey a feeling that you're more intelligent than your sisters, or at least you consider yourself so.

Chekhov, letter to Olga Knipper, 21 Jan. 1901

The play was read in his presence. He tried to control his indignation and repeated several times, 'But what I have written is a farce'.

V.I. Nemirovich-Danchenko, 'Iz Proshlogo', quoted in E.D. Surkov, *Chekhov i Teatr* (Moscow, 1961), p.309

He was afraid of provincial life being exaggerated and caricatured, of his officers being turned into the usual heel-clickers with jingling spurs. He wanted us to play the parts of simple, charming, decent people in 'untheatrical' uniforms which looked as if they'd actually been worn. 'The services have changed, you know. They've become more cultured, and many of them are even beginning to understand that their peace-time role is to carry culture into out-of-the-way places.'

K.S. Stanislavsky, 'A.P. Chekhov in the Art Theatre', quoted in E.D. Surkov, *Chekhov i Teatr* (Moscow, 1961), p.279

Chekhov wrote for orchestra. He is the nearest thing in literature to a symphonic composer. As long as he is acted as if he were a mixture of Ibsen, Maeterlinck, and sheer drivelling misery, he will be misrepresented, just as a composer would be misrepresented if all the instrumentalists were ignorant of the principles of counterpoint.

You could hardly have a more typical expression of Chekhov's dramatic genius than *The Three Sisters*. . . .

But if actors miss their way in its psychological web they are bound to make the whole thing seem disjointed, tame, and incomprehensible. . . . There was a fairly universal timidity which took the form of remaining frigidly transfixed and comically gloomy and of letting words drop out of the mouth as though they were words which had been memorized but not understood.

Frank Swinnerton, *The Nation*, 13 Mar. 1920

In this play he endows the three sisters with a certain sad beauty. . . . At times one almost suffers in sympathy with that caged bird Irina, for ever longing for her Moscow. Beatrix Thomson . . . withered and dropped like a wan lily. Margaret Swallow represented the pathos of romance manqué in the unhappily married woman. A faded air of Gounod made her live for one moment passionately, and then the spirit seemed to die again. As Olga, Mary Sheridan, the high-school drudge in her prim costume of the 'seventies looked like a du Maurier drawing.

A.E.W., *The Star*, 17 Feb. 1926

If a parallel is to be sought in English life or literature it can only be with the family of Mr. Bennet. It astonishes even me who makes it, how little far is the cry here! . . .

One at least of the many things lying near [the play's] core is the havoc wrought in the sisters' hearts when the brigade leaves that small provincial Russian town. Alas! that Masha cannot follow her Vershinin as Lydia Bennet followed the —— shire Militia to Brighton! . . .

Is it reading too much into the play to suggest that there is an essential difference between Irina and Masha, that whereas Irina will not easily love again, Masha with her hummings and cogitabundities is only Lydia and Kitty Bennet drawn to tragic scale, and will love the very next officer who has the wit to dress up his proposals metaphysically? . . . She is wittier and therefore more volatile than Irina. Indeed in Masha I find a suspicion of Hedda

Gabler. . . .

Olga is the steadying point of the trio, never quite gay, yet never wholly sad. Of common everyday happiness Olga is to know nothing; she has overstood her market, and is not to marry, and she takes a brave view of what lies before her.

James Agate, *Sunday Times,* 17 Nov. 1935

Michel Saint-Denis, the producer, has turned this more than ever into a lunatic charade. You sense a grey Russian daybreak becoming weirdly countenanced with streaky clouds yellowed by a rising sun you are never allowed to see; and gradually an uncomfortable feeling steals over you that if there are any more the whole world − or Russia anyway − will blow up.

John Gielgud again gives the performance of the evening as Vershinin, and singularly smug he makes him. At first you think it is the glasses he wears and the beard, and then you see that the whole aura of the man's hypocrisy surrounds him.

John Grime, *Daily Express*, 29 Jan. 1938

How was M. Saint-Denis's production achieved? The answer is, first, by his understanding that, spiritually, Chekhov's supreme gift was to bring to the observation of character a most delicate sense of justice; therefore any exaggeration in the acting is fatal. And, secondly, by his never forgetting that, technically, Chekhov's method was to develop character and situation by means of a dialogue which follows the broken rhythms of life, and by making every remark, every gesture of his characters, reflect the influence of group relations at the moment. This method can only be interpreted by all characters on the stage never ceasing to act, however trivial their contribution to the scene. It needs the most sensitive attention to detail. Those subtle touches! The passages of high emotion cannot escape anyone, but to relish this performance completely you must look out for those touches. The expression of shy embarrassment, almost envy, on Olga's face when she turns her back on the passionate last embraces between Vershinin and her sister; the radiant patronage on the faces of those two when they have just discovered their love, betrayed, too, in their voices, while the Baron is holding the stage on the theme that life must always be the same; the way Solyony instinctively seeks the mirror in a room, and how Kuligin, even in the last act, stoops down to mend a water-pipe.

Desmond MacCarthy, *New Statesman*, 5 Feb. 1938

John Gielgud . . . as Vershinin, spends as much ceremony and care upon the adjustment of his pince-nez as a priest might upon the donning of cassock, surplice and stole. Apart from this, however, this is an interesting performance and it is pleasant to see him attacking so vigorously a part for which he is fundamentally unsuited. The scenes with Masha are unconvincing for he seems not to understand how a man behaves who is desperately in love; but his long, wearisome discourses on the Future and the Chekhovian Utopia it promises were given with the simple, unconscious ponderousness of the true bore. The endless story of his wife and two little girls (none of whom appear) was song-plugged so neatly than nobody could fail to be aware that they were the three dullest people living. . . .

As for Michael Redgrave, his performance of Baron Nicolai was a living proof that you *can* eat your cake and have it. Throughout he played Irina's lover as a buffoon, something comic and pitiable but withal so endearing that he made her capitulation seem not only inevitable but a consummation to be desired. His leave-taking was one of the most moving pieces of acting I have seen for years.

P.T., *New English Weekly*, 10 Feb. 1938

Peter Ustinov contends that team-work and Chekhov are, in acting terms, incompatible. The characters, he maintains, are all soloists who occasionally interrupt each other's monologues but never listen to what anyone else is saying. They are deaf and blind to the world outside them − which is why they are funny and also why they are appalling. Fair comment, and in *Three Sisters*, a much more complex work than *The Cherry Orchard*, this technique is carried as far as it can go without blowing the play centrifugally apart. The very theme is estrangement: a brief brushing of lips is as close as anyone ever gets to another's soul. Of the three girls yearning for Moscow, Olga will never marry, Masha has married badly, and Irina is cheated of marriage by a tragic duel. Their brother, Andrey, is yoked to a prolific and faithless shrew. Two nihilists look on: one active − the savage Solyony, who scents his hands because, like Lear's they smell of mortality − and the other passive: Chebutikin, the doctor, jilted by the girls' mother and now drunk past caring. And so all sit, mourning and mumbling, making out of their inconsequence a choral lament on human isolation.

The Moscow production, based on the original staging by Nemirovich-Danchenko, gets all of this and infuses it with that strange dynamic apathy that is Chekhov's greatest demand on his actors. . . . M. Gribov's Chebutikin, in particular, is all I had heard of it; encrusted with corruption, a ponderous fish-eyed shrug of a man, he is yet capable, while remembering his dead love, of a sudden and transfixing pathos. The last act is, I suppose, the high-water mark of twentieth-century drama, yet this superb company meets its challenge as if opening the door to an old friend. The sound-effects and lighting are brilliant throughout: we weep, apart from anything else, for a lost world so lovingly revived. How these actors eat; and listen; and fail to listen; and grunt and exist, roundly and egocentrically exist!

Kenneth Tynan, *A View of the English Stage* (London, 1975), p.242-4

Anyone can play the lines in Chekhov; it takes an artist to play the pauses. An observation inspired by William Gaskill's current production of *The Three Sisters* which is winged to the public's attention starring Marianne Faithfull; she, of long yellow tresses and golden disc fame; a pop-singer Irina. What could be fancier? . . .

The play is woefully undercast — which is another way of saying the actors simply aren't up to its demands. But the real flaw, as in every Chekhov I've ever seen in this country, is that the cast is trying to capture some curious sense of 'Russianness' to which they feel the play belongs. Hence, speeches about the rosy future and the sorrowful past, about lost love and soured hope, all seem aimed at some feeling beyond the personal know-ledge of the performers. Instead of anglicizing the play, i.e., playing through the blood and bones of their own personal English experience, they Slavify the play. Not overtly by turning on stock Russian manners, but subtly, almost imperceptibly, by pretending that things like this happen in a 'special way' to Russian characters. Hence the universality of Chekhov, the quality that makes him readily translatable into any language (common humanity, etc.), is unconsciously subverted. This is the most unnatural kind of naturalism the stage can perpetrate as it is based on a fallacious idea of what is natural to other people rather than what seems natural to oneself.

Charles Marowitz, *Confessions of a Counterfeit Critic* (London, 1973), p.128-9

Krejca's view of the play [for the Czech Theatre, Behind the Gate] is totally unsentimental. His Masha is a bit of a bitch, supercilious in company, caring for no-one until Vershinin comes along, offering besides his naturally dashing presence the chance, however second-hand, of a link with Moscow; Andrei has already sunk with pudgy complacency into provincial life years before we meet him, and in the last scene he seems not the slightest bit incongruous pushing the pram; Solyoni is a nasty little neurotic with smarmed hair and the thoughtless stare of an unpractised voyeur, just the type to commit licensed murder for no better reason than envy, and Chebutykin (Krejca himself, bulky, balding and self-effacing in the best actor-manager tradition — you can't tear your eyes away from him!) is no cuddly old uncle figure but an ungainly, inadequate onlooker, his helpless detachment summed up in one powerful stage-image in the last act when slumped in the garden swing which, with one spindly tree, comprises the scenery, he lolls grotesquely like some uniformed baby in its harness.

The comedy of the play is neither exaggerated nor diminished, but there is a boisterous quality in the playing which seems much closer to Chekhov's intention than our own traditionally awed approach. So Krejca's ending to the play cuts across the rhetoric which threatened to sink so many productions; when the news of the Baron's death is brought to Irina, the three sisters scurry headlong about the stage, clutching at each other and spinning in a near-hysterical dance which counterpoints the blaring military music of the departing soldiers. The effect is dazing when compared with, say, Olivier's statuesque grouping at the National, but essentially it is a more convincing solution of the play's most dangerously portentous moments.

Frank Cox, *Plays and Players*, July 1969, p.54-5

Jonathan Miller's production arrives in London transformed from a fine production into a great one; and the first in my experience that fully acknowledges the objective nature of the piece. To varying degrees, every other performance I have seen falls into the trap of presenting the action from the sisters' own viewpoint: three Grade-A girls, well equipped for life in Moscow but pathetically defeated by the mediocrity of provincial life and too high-minded to protect themselves against a wastrel brother and his ruthlessly acquisitive wife.

Miller questions all this. The sisters are always sneering about the town, but what do they know about it as they entertain no society outside the officers' mess? They gush idealistically about work, but when they get a job they do nothing but complain of boredom and headaches. Masha has married a local schoolmaster, but does all she can to ignore him. As for the usually villainous intruder, Natasha, the worst one can say about her is that she knows exactly what she wants. It is not her fault that she cannot speak five languages: in fact, as the sisters' cultural horizon contracts, so Natasha's expands, and by the end of the play she is speaking passable domestic French and making headway with *The Maiden's Prayer*, and what is wrong with her affair with Protopopov if Masha is permitted to entertain Vershinin? . . .

What is true of all these General's children is that none of them possesses any courage. John Shrapnel's Andrey takes it out viciously on class inferiors, but succumbs to pathetic guilt among his equals. Susan Engel's Olga puts a protective arm around the old servant, but withdraws it and stands mutely abashed when Natasha orders her out of the room. Angela Down's Irena, the most selfless performance, renounces all the accustomed lyricism and presents from the start a character incapable of love; a dogmatic adolescent, charming only when she reverts to childhood, and greeting the news of the Baron's death with a rasped 'I knew it', as though a picnic had been rained off. . . .

Nowhere does the sense of paralysis appear more openly than in the Masha/Vershinin relationship. Nigel Davenport and Janet Suzman project the full intensity of the attraction, but it is clear that neither of them intends to do anything about it. Vershinin's philosophizing on the future comes over as a deliberate strategy for letting the present take its course; while Miss Suzman, a hunched figure, hands usually buried deep in her skirt pocket, appears armour-plated in self-sufficiency. . . . Since its opening, the choreography has developed amazingly: witness the speed and complexity of the interrupted party, with Masha executing a wild scarf dance and June Ritchie's Natasha covering every corner of the room with her officious clockwork strut, tapping on shoulders until she has brought the fun to a stop.

Irving Wardle, *The Times*, 24 June 1976

At the end of *The Three Sisters* last night there were flowers, tears shed by the many Russians present, and ten curtain calls. As you know, the play is another of Chekhov's pessimistic studies of the beaten people, the average people who live marred, stunted, unrealized existences, struggling weakly with a lonely, dull environment. . . .

We suspect that they became a bit stupefied by the prevailing inaction. Even when the Colonel (Mr. Stanislavsky), making love to the married and dissatisfied Masha (Mme. Chekhova) is informed of his wife'e endeavour at suicide, there is not much stir.

And later, as the town is burning down, the sisters and their household seem disinterested in the conflagration, since they lie around and continue to think and to talk about themselves. . . . It seems just another wearying item in *The Three Sisters* catalogue of lassitudes. . . .

We liked Mr. Stanislavsky in that hopeful soliloquy which he delivered as a reverie, reclining, eyes closed, in his chair and seeming to improvise it to its ultimate dissonance. And Mme. Chekhova when she listened and listened, as if she had not been hearing it for twenty-five years. And, in fact, all the others when we chanced to set our eyes, if not our ears, on them. A peculiar thing about the Russian actors is that the most important of them can come into a room or leave it without theatrical emphasis. You suddenly discover that they are present or that they are absent. They move about in 'tremulous oscillations' like electric needles.

Percy Hammond, *New York Tribune*, 30 Jan. 1923

Never did a play seem more like a museum piece than *The Three Sisters* did last night. . . . In those dear dead days of the 'twenties. how we hugged to our hearts the delicious pessimism of the Russians who were already becoming very old hat in Russia! Even in our years of happy innocence, prior to 1914, the Russian soul seemed full of grandeur to us when it was displayed in the art of Chekhov. . . . Now, with Russian women in the trenches and many of our American women in war work from factory to bomber ferrying, . . . *The Three Sisters* conceived by Chekhov, even though expertly played by Miss Cornell, Judith Anderson, and Gertrude Musgrove, seem to be three completely uninteresting females whose aspirations are trivial and whose fate is unimportant.

Burton Rascoe, *New York World-Telegram*, 22 Dec. 1942

Leaving aside questions of talent — for Ruth Gordon as Natasha gives a striking, even terrifying performance that is nevertheless as injurious to the play's values as Miss Cornell's awkward and senti-mental Masha — the main difficulty is that American actors cannot understand why Chekhov called many of his plays comedies. To the American theatre mind, a play that culminates in disastrous events is, by definition, a tragedy; the murder in the last act gives the director his clue. If you add to this the fact that the characters are unhappy, it is plain sailing! The funereal note is struck in the opening speech and the play is driven — at a respectable speed —

to its last resting-place in the fourth act. . . .

Mme. Litvinoff (an Englishwoman) remarked to newspaper reporters that *The Three Sisters* is an absurd play about three grown-up women who spend four acts not going to Moscow when they have the price of the ticket. This description, though derogatory in intention, is perfectly exact. That is what the play is about, and the failure of the three sisters to get to Moscow (and indeed the whole nostalgic dream of Moscow) is not tragic, but pathetic, touching, absurd. . .

What is missed . . . is the comic element in the play. Chekhov's characters are both witty and amusing, and they have, in addition, a flickering awareness of the absurdity of their position, and inconsequent but nonetheless real irony which raises the whole problem from the level of action to the superior level of consciousness. It is Chekhov's peculiar use of modified soliloquy to treat the theme of self-consciousness that is his dramatic signature; Miss Cornell and most of her fellow actors handle these delicate passages as though they were either so many yards of plain expository material or interpolated operatic dirges.

Mary McCarthy, Partisan Review, X (1943), p.184-6

This is a great and lovely play, and its greatness and loveliness come through instead of being obstructed and whittled away as I remember them to have been in the grandiose Broadway production of a dozen years ago. For one thing, the play is correctly interpreted by its director, David Ross. He has managed to get rid, not only of the grandiosity (which, at Fourth Street, is rather easy), but also of all that mooning and swooning around that passes for Chekhovian acting in the Anglo-American theatre. It is made clear that the sisters are small-town girls, not Park Avenue hostesses in disguise. It is made clear that the orations on the glorious future reflect, not the author's optimism, but the sad futility of Vershinin and Tusenbach who speak them.

The outstanding individual performances are three, and one of them is turned in by a youngster, Peggy Maurer, as Irina, who brings with beauty and intensity a capacity for stillness and repose which most of her colleagues miss. . . . If it seemed odd to have cast one of the oldest actors as the young Andrei, Morris Carnovsky more or less justified the choice. If he was not fully credible as a boyish fiancé, . . . he portrayed the pains of modern cuckoldom later with a combination of respect and intensity thoroughly Chekhovian.

Eric Bentley, What is Theatre (Boston, 1956), p.53-6

The Cherry Orchard

Comedy in four acts.
Written: 1903–04.
First production: Moscow Art Th., 17 Jan. 1904 (dir. K.S. Stanislavsky and V.I. Nemirovich-Danchenko; des. V.A. Simov; with Olga Knipper as Ranevskaya and Stanislavsky as Gaev).
Revived: Volksbühne, Berlin, 1919 (dir. Friedrich Kayssler); Théâtre Marigny, Paris, Nov. 1954 (dir. Jean-Louis Barrault; with Madelaine Renaud as Ranevskaya and Barrault as Trofimov); Teatro Stabile di Roma, 1966 (dir. Luchino Visconti); Wurttembergisches Staatstheater, Stuttgart, 1968 (dir. Peter Zadek); Residenz Th., Munich, 1970 (dir. Rudolf Noelte); Piccolo Teatro, Milan, 1974 (dir. Giorgio Strehler); Th. Bouffes du Nord, Paris, 1981 (dir. Peter Brook).
First London production: Aldwych Th., 29 May 1911 (with Nigel Playfair as Semyonov-Pishchik and Harcourt Williams as Trofimov).
Revived: St. Martin's Th., 12 July 1920 (dir. Mme. Donnet; with Edith Evans as Charlotte and Felix Aylmer as Semyonov-Pishchik); Lyric Th., 25 May 1925 (dir. J.B. Fagan; with John Gielgud as Trofimov); Barnes Th., 28 Sept. 1926 (dir. Fyodr Komissarzhevski; with Charles Laughton as Yepikhodov and Martita Hunt as Charlotta); Old Vic Th., 9 Oct. 1933 (dir. Tyrone Guthrie; with Athene Seyler as Ranevskaya, Charles Laughton as Lopakhin, and Flora Robson as Varya); New Th., 28 Aug. 1941 (dir. Tyrone Guthrie; with Athene Seyler as Ranevskaya); Old Vic Th., 25 Nov. 1948 (dir. Hugh Hunt; des. Tanya Moisewitsch; with Edith Evans as Ranevskaya, Cedric Hardwicke as Gaev, and Robert Eddison as Trofimov); Lyric Th., Hammersmith, 21 May 1954 (dir. John Gielgud; with Gwen Ffrangcon-Davies as Ranevskaya and Trevor Howard as Lopakhin); Sadlers Wells Th., 15 May 1958 (Moscow Art Th. production, dir. Victor Stanitsyn); Aldwych Th., 14 Dec. 1961 (dir. Michel Saint-Denis; des. Farrah); Queen's Th., 5 Oct. 1967 (dir. Richard Cottrell); National Th., at the Old Vic, 24 May 1973 (dir. Michael Blakemore; with Constance Cummings as Ranevskaya and Michael Hordern as Gaev); National Th. at the Olivier, 14 Feb. 1978 (dir. Peter Hall, des. John Bury; with Dorothy Tutin as Ranevskaya, Ralph Richardson as Firs, Robert Stephens as Gaev, and Albert Finney as Lopakhin).
First New York production: Jolson's 59th St. Th., 22 Jan. 1923 (Moscow Art Th. production in Russian).

Revived: Bijou Th., 5 Mar. 1928 (J.B. Fagan's London produc-
tion); 14th St. Th., 14 Oct. 1928 (dir. Eve le Gallienne); New
Amsterdam Th., 6 Mar. 1933 (dir. Eve le Gallienne); National
Th., 25 Jan. 1944 (dir. Margaret Webster and Eve le Gallienne);
4th St. Th., 18 Oct. 1955 (dir. David Ross); Theatre Four,
14 Nov. 1962 (dir. David Ross); Lyceum Th., 19 Mar. 1968
(dir. Eve le Gallienne; with Uta Hagen as Ranevskaya);
Anspacher Th., 11 Jan. 1973 (dir. Michael Schultz).
First published: 1904.
Translations: trans. M.S. Mandel (New Haven, 1908); in *Two
Plays by Tchekof,* trans. George Calderon (London, 1912); in
Plays by Anton Tchekoff, Second Series, trans. Julius West
(New York, 1916); in *The Moscow Art Theatre Series of
Plays,* trans. Jennie Covan (New York, 1922); in *Plays from
the Russian, Vol. I,* trans. Constance Garnett (London, 1923);
trans. Herbert Butler (London, 1934); trans. Kenneth James
(London, 1943); trans. Stark Young (New York, 1947); in
Anton Chekkov: Plays, trans. Elisaveta Fen (Harmondsworth,
1959); in *Anton Tchekhov: Plays and Stories,* trans. S.S.
Koteliansky (London, 1967); in *Chekhov: The Major Plays,*
trans. Ann Dunnigan (New York, 1964); in *Masterpieces of the
Russian Drama Vol. 2,* trans. C.C. Daniels and G.R. Noyes
(New York, 1961); in *Anton Chekhov: Four Plays,* trans.
David Magarshack (London, 1970); in *Oxford Chekhov III;*
in *Anton Chekhov's Plays,* trans. E.K. Bristow (New York,
1977); trans. Michael Frayn (London, 1978); version by
Trevor Griffiths, trans. Helen Rappaport (London, 1978).

*A sequence of unfortunate events, including the death of her
husband and seven-year-old son, has driven Lyubov Ranevskaya
from her Russian estate to France, where she has taken up with a
lover, been abandoned, and fallen into a miserable emigré life-style.
The play opens in the old nursery, on the spring morning of her
return to the estate, accompanied by her daughter, Anya, and
Anya's eccentric governess, Charlotta. A maidservant awaits
the party from the station with Lopakhin, the son of a former
serf, now a successful merchant. Soon after Ranevskaya's arrival,
she and her aristocratic brother, Gayev, are informed by Varya
(Ranevskaya's adopted daughter and housekeeper) that the estate,
which is hopelessly in debt and which has only the beauty of its
unproductive cherry orchard to recommend it, is up for sale.*

Lopakhin, the practical businessman, explains a plan he has to save the estate which would involve cutting down the orchard and selling off the land as building plots for summer villas. The fastidious brother and sentimental sister will have none of it. Act two takes place near sunset in the open countryside on the edge of the estate, and as Gayev addresses the setting sun a mysterious sound, like a breaking string, startles and frightens members of the group. The third act begins with the music and dancing of a party on the evening of the day on which the estate is being auctioned, until Lopakhin arrives and announces that he has bought it, together with the cherry orchard. The last act opens on a cold October day following the August of the sale: the nursery is stripped bare except for a few pieces of furniture and suitcases. Ranevskaya is returning to her repentant French lover, and Gayev is going to work in a bank. Firs, the old family retainer, has been taken ill and, it is thought, been removed to hospital. After brother and sister have bid a tearful farewell to the house, the silence is suddenly broken by the distant sound of an axe striking a tree, followed by the ghostly sound of shuffling feet. Firs appears in the dim light of the shuttered room: muttering to himself, he slowly lies down and remains motionless. Then, the sound like a breaking string is heard again, dying away in the distance.

What's turned out isn't a drama, but a comedy, in places even a farce. . . .

> Chekhov, letter to M.P. Alexeyeva (Lilina), 15 Sept. 1903

The last act will be joyful, just as the entire play is happy and frivolous.

> Chekhov, letter to Olga Knipper, 21 Sept. 1903

The fourth act of my play will be thin in content compared with the other acts, but effective.

> Chekhov, letter to Olga Knipper, 23 Sept. 1903

Oh, if only you could play the governess in my play! It's the best part; I don't like the rest.

> Chekhov, letter to Olga Knipper, 29 Sept. 1903

You will play Lyubov Ranevskaya as there isn't anybody else. She doesn't dress lavishly, but with great taste. She's an intelligent, very decent person, absent-minded, is kind to everyone and always has a smile on her face. . . . It's an old manor house where people once lived in style and this must be felt in the setting. Rich and comfortable. Varya's a bit crude and stupid but very good-hearted.

Chekhov, letter to Olga Knipper, 14 Oct. 1903

I was most worried about the static quality of the second act and a certain unfinished quality about the student Trofimov. You see Trofimov is in exile from time to time, and now and again thrown out of university, but how can these things be represented?

Chekhov, letter to Olga Knipper, 19 Oct. 1903

Nemirovich . . . has already sent me a telegram which describes Anya as being like Irina [in *Three Sisters*]. . . . but Anya is as much like Irina as I'm like Burdzhalov [an actor of roles such as Sir Andrew Aguecheek]. Anya is first and foremost a child, happy to the end, who has no awareness of life and isn't at all tearful, apart from in Act 2, where she only has tears in her eyes.

Chekhov, letter to Olga Knipper, 21 Oct. 1903

Anya doesn't cry once and never speaks in a tearful voice. She has tears in her eyes in Act 2 but her tone is happy and lively. Why do you talk in your telegram of all the crybabies in the play? Where are they? There's only one – Varya – and she is tearful by nature but her tears mustn't arouse a depressing feeling in the spectator. You'll often come across the indication 'through tears' in my stage directions but this is only an indication of the character's mood not one of tearfulness. There isn't a graveyard in the second act.

Chekhov, letter to Nemirovich-Danchenko, 23 Oct. 1903

No, I never wanted to make Ranevskaya into someone who had calmed down. Death alone can calm such a woman. . . . It is not difficult to act Ranevskaya. All you've got to do is to strike the right note from the outset; think up a smile and a manner of laughing and know how to dress.

Chekhov, letter to Olga Knipper, 25 Oct. 1903

It's true Lopakhin is a merchant, but he's a decent person in every sense and his behaviour must be that of a completely dignified and intelligent man, with nothing petty about him, without tricks, and I thought that this role, which is central to the play, would be brilliantly played by you. . . . In choosing the actor for this part you mustn't lose sight of the fact that Lopakhin was loved by Varya, a serious and religious girl, who wouldn't fall in love with someone who was just a rich peasant.

Chekhov, letter to Stanislavsky, 30 Oct. 1903

Charlotta talks good not fractured Russian — only she sometimes converts the soft sign into a hard sign at the ends of words and mixes up her masculine and feminine adjectival endings. Pishchik is a Russian, crippled with gout, old age and over-eating. He is stout and dressed in a peasant's sleeveless coat (*à la* Simov) in high boots without heels. Lopakhin wears a white waistcoat and yellow shoes, waves his arms about when he walks, takes broad strides and meditates while on the move — walks in straight lines. His hair is not short and for this reason he has to keep tossing back his head; when he's thoughtful he strokes his beard from back to front, i.e. from underneath the chin towards the mouth. Trofimov is clear I think. Varya has a black dress and a wide belt.

Chekhov, letter to Nemirovich-Danchenko, 2 Nov. 1903

The house is a large two-storied one. . . . [It] has to be large and solid: made of wood or stone, it doesn't matter which. It is very old and of enormous size of a kind which holiday makers don't rent but pull down and use the materials to build summer cottages. The furniture is old-fashioned, stylish, and solid; their financial straits and debts haven't affected the furnishings.

Chekhov, letter to Stanislavsky, 5 Nov. 1903

Dunya and Yepikhodov stand in Lopakhin's presence and don't sit down. Lopakhin is very much at ease, behaves like a lord of the manor and is on familiar 'thou' terms with the servants. They use the unfamiliar 'you' form when addressing him.

Chekhov, letter to Stanislavsky, 10 Nov. 1903

Konstantin Sergeyevich wants to bring in a train in Act 2, but I think it would be better to restrain him. He also wants frogs and corn-crakes. . . .

Chekhov, letter to Olga Knipper, 23 Nov. 1903

Lulu and K.L. [relations of Knipper's] saw *The Cherry Orchard* in March; both say that Stanislavsky acts revoltingly in Act 4, that he drags everything out painfully. How terrible! An act which should last a maximum of twelve minutes lasts forty in your production. I can only say one thing: Stanislavsky has ruined my play. Ah, well, let him get on with it.

Chekhov, letter to Olga Knipper, 29 Mar. 1904

Though Anton Chekhov's comedy may be a harmonious work of art, presented at home in its own atmosphere before people who know all about, if they do not actually live, the life it depicts, Mrs. Edward Garnett's *Cherry Orchard* cannot but strike an English audience as something queer, outlandish, even silly. . . . [The characters] all seem children who have never grown up. Genuine comedy and scenes of pure pathos are mixed with knock-about farce.

The Times, 30 May 1911

Unfortunately, the leading character, entrusted to Miss Katharine Pole, was interpreted in the wrong key. A magnetic woman, a *grande dame*, should have been chosen for this part. Miss Pole's style is that of *noli me tangere* — how dare you, and very theatrical at that. A fine performance was given by Mr. Franklin Dyall as the unmarried brother of the heroine, the kind of Russian so well known on the boulevardes, man of the world, great talker, great idler, sucking pastilles all day long, and playing the prince with empty pockets. A character, to a very comic degree and very well observed, was the ever-indebted gentleman-borrower of Mr. Nigel Playfair. Forcible was the rough-and-ready merchant of Mr. Herbert Bunston. Mr. Harcourt Williams rendered the student in that reflective and effective manner which we are wont to associate with Russian revolutionists in the bud. Miss May Jerrold was a restrained and almost pathetic milksister, who chooses to remain a pauper because the rich *parvenu* has not the courage to claim her willing 'yes'. On the whole, the performance was well directed, and it is nobody's fault that you cannot make Muscovites of Englishmen.

J.T. Grein, *Sunday Times*, 4 June 1911

I do not think it is a great play. But it is an intensely original and interesting play. I do not agree with any of the criticisms which have been passed upon it. It has a theme, and a perfectly plain theme — the break-up of an estate and of a family. It has a plot, and the plot is handled throughout with masterly skill. It is simply crammed with character. Indeed, it has so much character-ization, and unfamiliar characterization, that an unimaginative audience could not project itself beyond the confusing externalities of the characterization into the heart of the play. The second act is the least diverting. The first, third and fourth have not a weak moment. The close (more generally praised than any other part of the play) is perhaps somewhat over-theatrical for my realistic taste. . . . It is one of the most savage and convincing satires on a whole society that was ever seen in the theatre.

Arnold Bennett ('Jacob Tonson'), *New Age*, 8 June 1911

One looks on at the performance of this play, a little befogged, perhaps, by the first act, with a sensation that one is witnessing a vague and incoherent and trivial thing. Observe how characters wander in and out of the scene in a purposeless fashion. The old servant, Firs, stands about, muttering senilely to himself, while his master, Gaev, makes imaginary shots at billiards, or begins a rhetorical flourish. Madame Ranevskaia dribbles her fortune away without knowing that she is doing so, and Lopakhin, articu-late enough at bidding for an estate, becomes mum when a proposal of marriage should be made. Everything is inconclusive, invertebrate, supine, and yet how amazingly satisfying it is! . . .

The performance, on the whole, was admirable. . . . There is an identity between the circumstances of Madame Ranevskaia and any lady of the governing class in Ireland during the last thirty or forty years which should have made her an easy study for Miss Irving. . . . The finest performance in the play was by Mr. Ernest Paterson as Firs, the manservant, as rich a study of faithful senility as I have ever seen.

St. John Ervine, *The Observer*, 18 July 1920

It is, as a rule, when a critic does not wish to commit himself or to trouble himself, that he refers to atmosphere. And, given time, something might be said in greater detail of the causes which pro-duced this atmosphere — the strange dislocated sentences, each so erratic and yet cutting out the shape so firmly, of the realism, of the humour, of the artistic unity. But let the word atmosphere be taken literally to mean that Chekhov has contrived to shed over us a luminous vapour in which life appears as it is, without veils, transparent and visible to the depths. Long before the play was over, we seemed to have sunk below the surface of things and to be feeling our way among submerged but recognizable emotions. 'I have no proper passport. I don't know how old I am; I always feel I am still young' – how the words go sounding on in one's mind – how the whole play resounds with such sentences, which reverberate, melt into each other, and pass far away out beyond everything! In short, if it is permissible to use such vague language, I do not know how better to describe the sensation at the end of *The Cherry Orchard*, than by saying that it sends one into the street feeling like a piano played upon at last, not in the middle only but all over the keyboard and with the lid left open so that the sound goes on.

Virginia Woolf, New Statesman, 24 July 1920

The piece calls for the finest playing, and Mr. Fagan's company were often very fine. Miss Mary Grey, though physically too magnificent, subdued her soul to the required degree of slightness, and her pose in the second act and dumb grief in the third were lovely. . . . I am just a little bothered about the Gayef of Mr. Alan Napier and the Lopakhin of Mr. Fred O'Donovan. Was Gayef a trifle too seedy for a remnant of the old nobility? Was Lopakhin a wee bit too brutal? Mr. O'Donovan gave him a red-handed, destructive shade, whereas I suggest that he, too, belongs to the old order and will pass away with it. His cry of 'Strike up, music!' is ironical, not triumphant. He is ashamed of his success and would drown in. . . .

Mr. John Gielgud's Perpetual Student was perfection itself, Mr. Smith's Pishtchik was immensely jolly, and Mr. Clarence's Firs must have drawn tears from the policeman in the gallery. . . . I suggest that *The Cherry Orchard* is one of the great plays of the world. . . .

James Agate, Sunday Times, 31 May 1925

On its first production in London *The Cherry Orchard* seemed a lugubrious affair. The comic element was submerged. Mr. Tyrone Guthrie has not repeated the mistakes of Mr. Fagan, but in his determination to bring out the farcical extravagance of the dialogue and to dispel the notorious Russian gloom he has swung perilously near the other extreme and abated somewhat the deep pathos of the play. . . .

In a theatre so vast as the Old Vic he has had to broaden his effects, and the process is one which enforces penalties in Chekhov. Trofimov, the eternal student, dashing in distracted agony from his scene with Madame Ranevsky, falls downstairs, but because the scene itself has been played at a pace which slurred over its emotional significance the anti-climax has no more than its pure farcical value. Several of the best scenes are thus thrown away, and thrown away, it seems, because they are played too swiftly.

Another weakness lies in the performance of Miss Athene Seyler as Madame Ranevsky. She is delightful, but delightful in the wrong way. She seems much too sensible for the woman on whose feckless and emotional temperament the security of the cherry orchard depends. If the whole play cannot be built up round her character, it lacks unity. . . .

Mr. Charles Laughton's Lopahin, a loutish fellow, with head held on one side and flapping hands, is a very precise study of character, and though his practical mind brings him a sense of triumph, we are made to feel the self-distrust that lurks within. Miss Flora Robson also discovers the full significance of the eternal 'wallflower', suggesting the hardness of the ageing spinster and the hopeless passion from which the hardness springs.

The Times, 10 Oct. 1933

Athene Seyler gave a lighter reading of the character of Lyubov Andreyevna, the orchard's spendthrift owner, than we are accustomed to. The emphasis she laid on the lady's flightiness prevented us from believing very deeply in her emotional scenes. The interpretation was, however, completely consistent within itself, and beautifully performed.

W.A. Darlington, *Daily Telegraph*, 10 Oct. 1933

Mr. Tyrone Guthrie's production of *The Cherry Orchard* is first-rate. . . . Nostalgia, too much nostalgia is the danger that threatens every producer of *The Cherry Orchard* if the savage critical core of Chekhov's work is ignored: between the lovely opening when Mme. Ranevska and her daughter Anya return just before dawn to the old family house after their long railway journey . . . and the last departure with the dust-sheets on the furniture, the shrouded rocking-horse, the old servant forgotten, and the sound of the cherry trees falling under the axe. . . . Chekhov's work is not for the young: it is as old as the strange land from which it emerged: it is bleached with the doctor's memory of cholera, of interminably suffering peasants; twisted by sickness, boredom reels towards Yalta to die. . . .

Watch the eternal student (interestingly made-up to look like Chekhov himself and very well acted by Mr. Walter Hudd) scratch his bottom while he boasts about mankind. See the tired broken Gaev lift his nose like an old war-horse at the click of billiard balls, and in the last scene the absurd governess, Charlotta, sprawl like a discarded ventriloquist's doll in the corner of the about-to-be-abandoned room. It is these little moments, flashes of individual insight, which make a play fresh however often we see it.

Graham Greene, *The Spectator*, 5 Sept. 1941

Gielgud's new production put the play back into its realistic Russian setting. . . . It is right to stress the humour (Tchehov himself did so), but now the sadness, too, came through tenderly, in sudden quietudes of heartache broken only by the twanging of a guitar, the song of birds greeting the dawn. . . .

Gwen Ffrangcon-Davies seemed born to play Mme. Ranevsky, on whose warmth, spendthrift generosity, and fecklessness the pattern of the play hinges. One believed in her quicksilver changes of mood, the grief that pierced her sudden delights. Esme Percy, though truly beyond the age for Leonid Gaev, gave an endearing display of affection and misplaced eloquence, Pauline Jameson was a moving Varya, George Howe a delightful Pistchik (that Russian Micawber whose 'something' surprisingly *does* turn up), and Robert Eddison the most drole receiver of Epihodoff's 'misfortunes' one remembers. Trevor Howard as Lopahin played finely the key scene in which – a little drunk, half-elated, half-ashamed – he reveals he has bought the estate on which his ancestors worked as serfs.

Audrey Williamson, *Contemporary Theatre 1953–1956*
(London, 1956), p.147-8

Compared with English productions the lighting [of the Moscow Art Theatre production] alone is as brilliant in impact as the primary colours hitting one for the first time from a masterpiece recently cleaned. . . . In *The Cherry Orchard* the tree tops, loaded with blossom and translucent behind crystalline windows, join with a room very sparingly furnished and a dawn as bracing as the opening act of *Oklahoma*! to weigh the scales heavily on the side of youth. Anya, a coltish schoolgirl with pigtails, is at home in this room, more than anyone else. After all, it is still called the nursery. . . .

But certain aspects of this version are questionable. In flat contradiction to the 'oppressive sense of emptiness' asked for in his stage directions to the last act, the set looks even gayer when its meagre furnishings are covered up . . . and in the only movement undeniably external to Chekhov, Anya and Trofimov strike an attitude made reminiscent of propaganda posters as they make their final exit. Still, explicitly in the text, she does say goodbye to the old life and he greets the new. The lines ask for attitudes, though perhaps not that one. Then bronzed workmen are glimpsed outside, closing the shutters and leaving Firs to die in a room gently dappled with sunbeams through the apertures. It is as benign a stage death as you ever saw, mellow Shakespearian Chekhov.

If there are some brash lighting and scenic effects hardly to be expected from the 'austere' M.A.T., the sound effects are astounding. Instead of a few apologetic chirps . . . there is an all-out dawn chorus and later a solo from a cuckoo. . . . As for the mysterious sound of a string snapping 'as if out of the sky' . . . it is deep, plangent, and in context disturbing beyond imagination. Considered side by side with the decor and lighting, the use of sound leads one on to the impression of virile energy — conveyed at times with an almost childish directness as when the clumsy Yepikhodov collides with a doorpost — which impregnates the M.A.T.'s acting. . . .

For violent impact Lopakhin's assumption of ownership . . . is a case in point. Following Chekhov's expectation that Stanislavky would choose the part for himself, and his reminder that Varya would not love a boor, Lukyanov plays him for the first two acts in a respectable loose-limbed, restless way, exasperated, kind, and impatient. Getting things done in this environment, he lets us know, is like swimming in treacle, the more frustrating the better your normal rhythm. After the sale he comes in unobtrusively and sits quietly on a settee. What sets him off is Varya's action in throwing the keys on the floor, and to mark this she does not just toss them down, but crashes them down directly in front of her, centre stage, with an overarm movement. Alone with Ranevskaya, he begins his triumphant tirade sitting down, rises after a few lines as if lifted by his own mounting emotion and picks the keys up. He throws them a yard or so in the air and catches them, right-handed in a movement like a punch which carries his whole body up stage towards the ballroom; he storms into it through the first of two arched openings in the wall.

Inside the ballroom he halts, well in view of the audience through the aperture, and orders the band to play. The pause before it obeys is agonizing. When the music starts, Ranevskaya, who until now has held a monumental 'freeze' while seated on the chair she reached out for on hearing the news, and is alone on the main stage, begins to weep. Lopakhin breaks something in the ballroom with a violence in tune with the sacking of the Czar's palace and comes into full view again, a tall man holding high on to both sides of the second aperture. We see him there, a few yards behind Ranevskaya, wild-eyed and panting, bestially dominant though limp from the emotional effort, until the woman's misery seems to restore his humanity as a sense of guilt. He staggers miserably into the room and to the opposite side of the table against which she is sitting, like a child seeking reassurance after doing something outrageous. She does not even look at him.

This episode illustrates, among other things, Chekhov's organic use of the stage, including spatial build-up of dynamic movement and use of props every bit as important as the dialogue, and confirms that if Stanislavsky had not existed it would have been necessary to invent him.

Laurence Kitchin, 'Chekhov without Inhibitions: the Moscow Art Theatre in London, 1958', in *Mid-Century Drama*, (London, 1960) p.133-8

To see *The Cherry Orchard* well played is to crystallize one's random impressions a good deal. Despite the melancholy of its conclusion, it is, indeed, comedy, as Chekhov always maintained. Moreover, it is clearly the apotheosis of Chekhovian drama, finer, deeper than *Three Sisters* – a myriad of human light and shade. And its unobtrusive symbolism becomes articulate in Anya's joyous enthusiasm for the 'new life' and the contented death of the 'old life' in Firs, muttering resignation while the woodsmen hack at the cherry trees, singing at their labours, and the servants firmly close the shutters from the outside. What complete finality there is in that gradually expiring conclusion! With his last curtain Chekhov sealed an epoch.

Brooks Atkinson, *New York Times,* 18 Nov. 1928

Without drawing from *The Cherry Orchard* the social and economic morals which latter-day supporters of the new Russian political order most cherish, the piece is such a poignant allegory of futility played in terms of almost fantastic ingenuousness that the observer has no difficulty in imagining at least some of the reasons for the decline of the old Russian scheme of things on a far more comprehensive scale than that embraced by the childlike and footlessly gentle family with which the play is concerned.

Lucius Beebe, *New York Herald-Tribune*, 7 Mar. 1933

Part of the difficulty in the present production lies in its casting. Miss Le Gallienne, while presenting a spirited, indeed, a 'spirituelle' silhouette, seems more like a reincarnation of La Parisienne than of the tender, laughing, warm-hearted, and irresponsible creature of Chekhov's imagining. There is a sharpness and intelligence about Miss Le Gallienne's Mme. Ranevsky that makes her feckless conduct inexplicable as well as inexcusable. . . . She moves with authority, with a kind of spirited grace, even though she does not at any point capture the elusive, mercurial essence of that temperament which can move with lightning speed from tears to laughter, which can compass joy and despair in a single breath.

Joseph Schildkraut as Gayev, Mme. Ranevsky's ineffectual brother, has built a detailed, highly elaborated, humorous portrait, not quite caricature but tending in that direction. In fact . . . this production emphasizes the humorous idiosyncrasies of character with which the play abounds. As a result, the production as a whole lacks cohesion and line. . . . Stefan Schnabel's performance is perhaps typical of the method used here. Externally he is right for the part. He is large, lumbering, moving with the awkwardness Chekhov suggests when he says that Lopahin swings his arms from the shoulders when he walks. Schnabel has the outward appearance of the peasant-turned-merchant, yet he never convinces you that he really understands the springs of Lopahin's being, the mixture of humility and pride, of passion and arrogance that makes him destroy the people he loves and admires; leads him to triumph coarsly over their defeat, but prevents him from proposing marriage to one of their number.

Rosamond Gilder, *Theatre Arts Monthly*, Apr. 1944, p.199-202

Chekhov's literary career proper is generally considered to date from 1886 and an influential letter which he received from the writer and critic D.V. Grigorovich. As a consequence of this, he felt prompted to take his own creative writing more seriously. His 'mature' literary phase is commonly seen to fall between 1888 and 1903, beginning with his long short story *The Steppe* and concluding with *A Marriageable Girl/The Betrothed* (Nevesta), published approximately six months before he died. This final phase consists of the 54 works which make up Volumes IV–IX of *The Oxford Chekhov* (1965–1980), translated and edited by Ronald Hingley.

According to tables calculated by Hingley and reproduced in his *A New Life of Chekhov* (1976), a total of 60 short stories belong to Chekhov's mature phase but, of these, Chekhov himself excluded six from his *Collected Works*. This still leaves an astonishing total of 528 stories regarded as belonging just to the 'early' period of Chekhov's writing. Any attempt to give a coherent synoptic account of Chekhov's non-dramatic output thus poses formidable problems because of its scale and variety.

He began writing when a medical student in Moscow and, by the end of 1884 (when he was 24), had published nearly 300 short pieces, under various pseudonyms, in several humorous magazines and newspapers produced in St. Petersburg and Moscow. Most of the work was done for the Petersburg weekly *Fragments (Oskolki)* and consisted, for the most part, of very brief items. He was not freed from the constraints of brevity until, in 1885, he was first accepted by the *Petersburg Gazette*, for which he went on to write more than 100 items in the course of three years. However, the major turning point in his literary career came when he was accepted by the more respectable 'thick journal' *New Times (Novoye Vremya)*, edited in St. Petersburg by A.A. Suvorin, which published Chekhov's work under his own name.

A group of early stories which are of particular relevance in the present context are those dealing with the theatre, six of which were published together as *Fairytales of Melpomene* in 1884. Some idea of what Chekhov thought of the theatre of his day can be gained from his depiction of members of the acting fraternity, who are usually drunken spendthrifts suffering from a surfeit of misplaced conceit. The perennial themes include bad theatre management; a general contempt for worthwhile plays and an exaggerated preference for the pretentious and third-rate; financial incompetence; and the absence of any feeling in the profession generally that theatre work might involve any sense of vocation.

Already by 1882, Chekhov had begun to turn his hand to more extended works, of which *Belated Blossom/Late-Blooming Flowers* is generally singled out as anticipating the style of his mature writing. The story is set against the wilting background of a dying aristocracy, which is contrasted with the tough Doctor Toporkov, who stems from a serf background, and is shown to survive in a manner which anticipates Lopakhin in *The Cherry Orchard* – although the price he pays in sacrificing human feeling for the sake of financial gain is, perhaps, closer to the fate of Doctor Startsev in *Ionych* (1898).

In common with most nineteenth-century writers, Chekhov had to live with state censorship, and learned his lesson fairly early in his career when his 'fairy tale' with a political theme, *To Talk or Not to Talk* (1884), was suppressed. It described an episode on a train journey during which one of the passengers, having talked indiscreetly with a travelling companion who turns out to be a plain-clothes security policeman, disappears for two years.

Another early worthwhile piece was also rejected for publication, on this occasion by Chekhov himself. *He Understood* (1883) is a tale of a poacher hauled before the local estate owner, who eventually lets him off with a caution when the peasant's account of his addiction to hunting puts the owner in mind of his own addiction to the bottle. The story contains some typically fine Chekhovian nature description, as well as a great deal of vivid detail, such as the description of a wasp trapped in the same room as the peasant as he awaits his interrogation.

Another group of early stories deals with a Gogolian world of clerks, petty bureaucrats, and minor government officials. One of the best known is *Death of a Government Clerk* (1883), in which a clerk visiting the theatre sneezes over the neck of an official sitting in front of him, who can't be bothered to listen to his apologies, either at the time, or later when the clerk calls on him at home. The clerk frets away and dies of anxiety. In *Fat and Thin* (1883), two old school friends meet unexpectedly on a station platform. The joy of the thinner turns to sycophantic grovelling when he learns that the other is ten grades higher than he is in the civil service 'table of ranks'.

Alongside stories of clerks who allow their bosses to sleep with their wives, or imitate the crowing of cocks to gain promotion, are stories of schoolmasters who, for Chekhov, tend to represent a repressed section of humanity. Of the pedagogues treated in *Slander* (1883) and *The Tutor* (1884), one is tortured by false rumours of his sexual activities, the other humiliated by having his intellectual shortcomings exposed. This group of stories anticipates the more substantial treatment of members of the teaching profession contained in *The Teacher of Literature/The Russian Master* (1894), and *The Man in a Shell/A Hard Case* (1898).

Chekhov's interest in the world of childhood also forms a significant part of his literary output during this earlier period. One of the first examples is *Oysters* (1884), an account of a starving child taken as a joke to a restaurant and invited to eat a meal of oysters, calculated to inspire nausea in equal proportion to the need to assuage the pangs of hunger. The idyllic aspect of childhood comes through in stories such as *The Cook's Wedding* (1885) and *A Day in the Country* (1886), where an impoverished shoemaker shares his love of the countryside with equally impoverished waifs, or even in a tale of disenchantment such as *An Everyday Trifle*, where a child whose parents are separated finds his faith in the adult world shattered.

Probably the best known of his stories involving children are *Sleepyhead* (1888) and *Vanka* (1886). The latter is told in epistolary form by a young peasant lad, Vanka, who writes a pathetic letter to his grandfather in which he recounts his feelings of homesickness and the miseries of separation. We finally realize that the touchingly written missive will never reach its destination as Vanka is too ignorant to know how to address the letter correctly. In *Sleepyhead*, an over-worked peasant girl smothers the crying infant she is supposed to be tending because its incessant noise is preventing her from sleeping. As the Soviet critic, Pyotr Bitsilli, has remarked, only certain writers in English come anywhere near Chekhov in his depiction of the world of the child — Kipling and Mark Twain. The same critic claims that Chekhov's ability to enter the world of animals is also unsurpassed by any writer other than Kipling, and cites his story about a dog, *Kashtanka* (1887), in support of this — 'the first *real* dog in world literature'.

This 'literature of commiseration', as it has been described, can be read alongside parodies and imitations of detective novels, such as *The Phosphorous Match/The Safety Match* (1884), satires on love and marriage, and brilliant genre sketches such as *The Bird Market/In Moscow on Trubnoy Square* (1883). Other stories concern the lives of professional people such as doctors and lawyers, the former usually shown to be altruistic, the latter commonly revealed as cynical and inured to human suffering.

The acting profession is represented once again by *The Tragic Actor* (1883), which describes the farcical elopement of a tragic actor and a rich man's daughter, which culminates in his beating her when her father fails to send them any money. Other early stories deal with the plight of wealthy landowners reduced to penury, either through alcoholism or through misfortunes financial or amorous. One of the best examples is *In Autumn* (1883), which Chekhov dramatized as *On the High Road*.

Another Chekhov interest, ecology, finds its way into an early tale such as *The Naive Wood Demon* (1884), while others reveal a strong feeling for human decency as well as the pathos of man's inhumanity to man. This is apparent even in a farcical story like *A Daughter of Albion* (1883), in which a Russian landowner fishing alongside his employee, a frigidly stiff English governess, strips stark naked in front of her before wading into the river to retrieve his hook, as if to demonstrate that she fails to exist for him as a human being, just as her failure to learn her employer's language is symptomatic of her complacent insularity.

Probably the most extraordinary work of this early phase is the only novel Chekhov ever wrote, *The Shooting Party* (1884–85), which was serialized in a Petersburg newspaper. In essence, it reveals Chekhov's interest in the kind of detective fiction which had become the stock in trade of station bookstalls in Russia after 1880, and produced imitations and parodies based primarily on the work of the popular French writer Gaboriau.

Despite the occasionally baroque extravagance of the narrative, the novel anticipates a great deal of what Chekhov later came to write. The relationship between some of the more melodramatic incidents and those of his play *Platonov* seem clear, as do elements of parody, such as the murder of the parrot by the narrator, who also turns out to be the murderer of Olga, the forester's daughter, and who, miraculously, remains unpunished at the end just as Vanya is seen to get away with the attempted murder of Serebryakov in *Uncle Vanya*.

A major phase of Chekhov's fiction writing is heralded by his story *The Huntsman* (1885), the central character of which has a passion for the chase which amounts almost to an artist's calling. The story dramatizes an eternal conflict in Chekhov's work between the world of nature and the constraints of the social world. An encounter on a country road between the huntsman and his wife reveals the extent of the distance between them. The tale concludes with the huntsman turning his back on domesticity in a symbolic union with the natural world as his receding figure merges with the landscape.

Many other stories from this phase of Chekhov's development deal with aspects of peasant life, such as the atmospheric piece *A Dead Body* in which two peasants, one of them the village idiot, are encountered at night by a superstitious pilgrim as they guard a corpse and await the arrival of the authorities. The harshness of peasant life is dealt with in *Sergeant Prishibeyev*, which concerns a paranoid bully who tyrannizes the peasants but then fails to understand why he is brought before the courts and given a month's sentence. Even as he is being taken away he bawls at the crowd of villagers to disperse, as he considers talking together in public to be a breach of the law.

A most moving story of human inadequacy and the suffering of poor people is *Sorrow* (1885), in which a woodturner, who has ill-treated his wife all their married life, is taking her to hospital by cart when they are caught in a blizzard. While driving around directionless (in a manner which has clear symbolic overtones) he notices that his wife has died. The event brings home to him what their life has been like and provokes a belated desire for atonement and a new beginning.

It was after 1885 that the influence of Tolstoy on Chekhov's work became most noticeable, and this influence lasted until about 1891. This was the period when Chekhov began to contribute to *New Times* and, 'Tolstoyanism' can be detected in the themes and treatment of many of the 21 pieces written between February 1886 and March 1887. *Agafya* (1886) and *The Witch* (1886) take as their subjects the sexually rapacious wives of a railway guard and a deacon, both of whom betray their husbands. Similarly, in *Slime/Mire* (1886), sexual passion is presented as both overpowering and inexplicable in the person of the slovenly Jewess who intoxicates by virtue of her sheer physical proximity. The final vision is of almost the entire male population of the district stuck in the 'slime' of her sexual attraction.

Other Tolstoyan themes such as non-resistance to evil and social salvation through faith in personal, spiritual revolution are apparent in *A Nightmare* (1886), which ends with a sermon on personal shame as well as extolling the virtues of useful social activity. The sense that it is human nature which is in need of spiritual care and attention is the theme of *Enemies* (1887), in which a doctor is called away from the bedside of his dead son to tend a woman who has had a heart attack. This turns out to have been a ruse to get her man out of the house so she can run away with her lover. The doctor vents his anger on the appalled, abandoned husband, little appreciating that the latter's distress is no less deserving of commiseration than is his own loss of a son.

One of the most impressive stories of this period is undoubtedly *Easter Eve* (1886), in which the narrator takes a ferry across a river to attend an Easter service. The beauty of the night, lit with fires, and the mystery and wonder of the service held in a monastery, is contrasted with the dominant image of the stoically suffering monk who works the ferry on a tow-rope endlessly from one side of the river to the other, mourning for the recent death of a fellow monk, his closest friend. Chekhov welds church language and religious myth closely together to create the strange poetic flavour of the narrative. A comparable feeling is conveyed in the story *In Passion Week* (1887), which, through the narrative of a nine-year-old child, conjures up the religious feeling of communion and confession, as well as the joy of absolution.

A major work of the same year is *The Kiss*, in which Chekhov begins to explore what was to become familiar territory, of absorbing interest to someone who was both a creative artist and a practising doctor – the borderline between fantasy and madness. A staff-captain, who is aware of his personal unattractiveness as well as being painfully shy, finds himself at a party in an unfamiliar town when he is kissed in the dark by a lady in mistake for her lover. The event has the effect of utterly transforming him, although the awakening, because it is based on illusion, brings destruction with it. A mistake both brings a human being to life and, simultaneously, makes life impossible to bear.

This mentally unstable aspect of human affairs is also dealt with in *Volodya* (1887), in which the central character, a schoolboy, is sexually awakened by losing his virginity to an older woman, a friend of his mother's. He is so disgusted and horrified that he commits suicide. In *A Nervous Breakdown/The Seizure* (1888), based on Chekhov's own experience of the Sobolev Street brothels in Moscow, a law student is introduced by two friends to the brothel quarter of the city and the horror and revulsion this produces leads to the breakdown of the title, and to consultation with a psychiatrist who cynically prescribes a remedy consisting of a mixture of bromide and morphine. The final comment, as usual, belongs to the world of nature as the snow sifts quietly and indifferently on the world and on Sobolev Street.

In *The Party/Name-Day Party* (1888), Chekhov chronicles the feelings and sensations of a female protagonist. The heroine, Olga, a person of liberal sentiments and a former college student, is oppressed by her domestic life, a feeling intensified by the fact that she is also in the later stages of pregnancy. Despite her condition, she takes on the organization of her husband's name-day party — a formal dinner, an island picnic, and a supper — all of which produces an emotional crisis at the end of the day. A quarrel with her husband leads to her premature confinement and the death of the baby. Chekhov described part of his intention in writing the story as 'one long protest against falsehood' as the surrounding world is seen through the increasingly alienated eyes of the pregnant woman.

Chekhov's major work of 1888, *The Steppe*, was preceded by other stories with a natural setting written while he was under the influence of several weeks travel in the Russian countryside. The first, *Happiness* (1887), describes a night spent in the steppes and introduces a moment when a strange noise disrupts the stillness, interpreted by a young shepherd as the sound of a tub breaking loose in the mineshafts — much as the sound of the breaking string in *The Cherry Orchard* is interpreted by Lopakhin. The atmospheric sound of panpipes in *The Shepherd's Pipe* also recurs at the end of the first act of that play.

The narrative technique of *The Steppe*, similar to that of *In Passion Week*, adopts the point-of-view of a nine-year-old boy, Yegorushka, who is being taken by his uncle from his native village to school in a distant city. The extended narrative covers eight chapters, each consisting of an episode in Yegorushka's journey during which, in Chekhov's words 'I depict the plain, mauve horizons, sheep drovers, Jews, priests, storms at night, inns, wagon-trains, steppe birds, etcetera'. The whole is a kind of tone poem of nature in which adventures and encounters enliven the descriptions of the constantly changing landscape.

The most significant long short story after *The Steppe* was *A Dreary Story* (1889), approximately 90 pages in length, about a Russian professor of medicine with an international reputation who begins to realize, as he approaches retirement, that an over-emphasis on intellectual life has starved his emotional relationships with others, especially with those closest to him such as his ward Katya and his daughter Liza. The 'vicious circle in which a kindly intelligent man can be trapped' (in Chekhov's words) is a ratio-cinative one, and is conveyed through the anguish the professor experiences over the absence of any ideal in life. This produces the long-drawn-out arguments of the narrative (which Chekhov considered essential while acknowledging the criticisms that they tended to be boring) about life in general, and on literature and the theatre in particular. Stoical and pessimistic themes are mooted in the references to Marcus Aurelius, Schopenhauer, and Shakespeare. In the end, Katya, who like Konstantin in *The*

Seagull has had a career in the theatre ruined for lack of a sense of direction, turns in desperation to the old man whom she has loved but finds that he is impotently incapable of offering her help or advice.

The post-Sakhalin phase of Chekhov's writing saw a reaction against a previously dominant Tolstoyanism. The first signs of this are already apparent in *Gusev* (1890), a grim story about two contrasting attitudes to life and death, in which two peasant soldiers, both of them dying, are being brought home by ship. The one rails against death and berates the other, Gusev, for his quietism and his tendency to face death with resignation and Tolstoyan humility. The serenity of Gusev's burial service is grotesquely counterpointed with the vision of a shark which rips the body from its sailcloth shroud as it sinks through the water.

In *The Duel* (1891), the longest story of Chekhov's maturity, running to some 160 pages, he finally breaks free of Tolstoy's influence (although the theme of human redemption from moral squalor still has a Tolstoyan ring to it). The central conflict is between the decadent Laevsky and the Darwinian zoologist, von Koren — the latter obsessed with the need to redress social evils and rationalizing his hatred of Laevsky along philosophical lines — although the basis of their conflict is Laevsky's treatment of his mistress, Nadezhda. According to von Koren, superfluous people like Laevsky threaten the doctrine of natural selection in diluting the strength of the human stock. Meanwhile, Nadezhda's infidelity with the police chief, Kirilin, produces a spiritual revolution in Laevsky, who sees her action as a reflection of his own moral failings. Finally, having been saved from almost certain death in a duel with von Koren by the deacon's timely warning shout, Laevsky watches as von Koren's boat leaves, battling with the incoming waves which produce a backwards movement for each forward advance — an image, seemingly, of man's eternal quest for the truth.

The Grasshopper/The Butterfly/The Flibbertigibbet (1892), also seems, on the surface, a kind of Tolstoyan moral fable, in which a frivolous woman, an amateur painter, marries a saintly, modest doctor and devotes her life to the search for greatness. She involves herself in an adulterous relationship with a second-rate artist, without realizing that the truly great man she is looking for is, in fact, her own husband. As a result of overwork, he carelessly infects himself with diphtheria and dies. Whilst mourning her loss, Chekhov makes it plain that the wife's superficial philistinism is unregenerate. The human qualities of the doctor, Dymov, his purposeful social activity, are in stark contrast to the feckless dilettantism of the world with which his wife associates.

These contrasts are undoubtedly intensified in Chekhov's own mind by the experience of his Sakhalin visit. Likewise, a view of the world as a version of a penal institution, as in *Ward No. 6* (1892), also seems coloured by the author's memory of the convict island. The central character, Dr. Ragin, is head of a 'zemstvo' hospital. Rather like Ivanov in the play, he has become discouraged in his attempts to effect reforms and has settled down into a mood of stoical boredom, comforting himself with readings from history and philosophy, especially the writings of Marcus Aurelius. This policy works quite well until he discovers an interesting madman in Ward No. 6, who has been driven into a state of paranoia by his sense of the world's injustice. Ragin begins to spend most of his time in fascinated conversation with this intelligent 'lunatic', until an ambitious subordinate exploits the opportunity to have Ragin declared insane and committed to the same ward as his patient. Here, the fists of Nikita the porter beat every last vestige of Ragin's quietist philosophy out of his head before he finally dies of a stroke. Chekhov's contemporary, the writer Leskov, felt prompted to state that 'Ward No. 6 is Russia'.

Between 1893 and 1895 women began to play an increasingly important role in Chekhov's life and in his writing. In *An Anonymous Story* (1893), a young woman deserts her lover for an anonymous revolutionary, only to discover that he has lost his revolutionary faith and merely wants her as his mistress. She poisons herself. In *A Woman's Kingdom* (1894), the central character is the lonely Anna, whose inheritance of a factory and considerable wealth is complicated by her working-class origins. The story focuses on the guilt she feels at profiting from the foundry, as well as on her desire to marry one of her workmen, which runs the risk of offending against social propriety. The whole amounts to a comment on the weakness of woman in a male-dominated society. While she cannot return to her roots, Anna is also prevented from entering the kind of society to which her wealth would normally entitle her.

In *The Teacher of Literature* (1894), the central character is Manya, who marries Nikitin, a local teacher who has worked himself up from poverty to become a respected person in the town. The anticipated idyll ends with the marriage ceremony as Nikitin descends into the bourgeois hell of marriage, poisoned by the banality of his wife and her relations. The picture is full of comic Gogolian detail, but the cumulative effect is horrific as

87

Manya fills the house, and even the marriage bed, with cats and dogs, while feeding the servants on scraps. The story ends with Nikitin making an entry in his diary in which he lists the horrors of domestic life while dreaming of escape before he is driven mad.

In *The Order of St. Anne/Anna on the Neck* (1895), a poor girl marries a rich civil servant who, as her benefactor, exacts obedience and gratitude. The wife discovers a power of her own at a ball given by her husband's superior and her sexual success with influential males leads to her husband being awarded the Order of St. Anne. Realizing that he now depends on her for social advancement, the husband whom she formerly feared to contradict is now treated with contempt as she simultaneously proceeds to turn her back on the symbol of her own social origins in the shape of her impoverished family.

Ariadne (1895) chronicles a man's changing reactions to the woman in his life, an extremely beautiful and desirable individual who uses men in a fairly unscrupulous fashion. The narrator, Shamochkin, tells of his relationship with Ariadne, whose impulsive selfishness charms him, of his eventual rejection by her, and of her flight to Europe into the arms of another. He concludes that women must be educated equally with men so that the extension of their intellectual interests may have the effect of curbing their primitive urge to dominate and assuage a preoccupation with their own existence as solely sexual beings.

The House with the Mezzanine/An Artist's Story (1896), also contains powerful portraits of female types in the contrasting figures of Lida and Misyus – the one strong and predatory, the other passive and vulnerable. Both live on an estate across which a landscape painter stumbles while out for a stroll: the artist falls in love with the younger, Misyus, and engages in hostile arguments with Lida, who is involved in political activity on the local council. The conflict between Lida and the artist has some of the overtones of the opposition between Laevsky and von Koren, between practical quasi-socialism and semi-religious quietism. The struggle between them is, however, essentially a struggle for the soul of Misyus, which Lida wins by sending her away.

Two stories of 1894, *The Black Monk* and *The Student*, appear somewhat anachronistic in this context. *The Student* is important because, according to Chekhov's friend the writer Ivan Bunin, Chekhov regarded the story as evidence that he possessed an optimistic outlook. Basically, it retells the story of Christ before the High Priests and of St. Peter's denial, as relayed with artless simplicity by a poor itinerant seminary student to a group he encounters around a camp fire on Good Friday eve. It concludes with the student going on his way with 'his soul filled with joy', while life 'seemed to him rapturous, marvellous, and full of lofty meaning'.

The theme of *The Black Monk*, by contrast, was suggested to Chekhov by a nightmare he experienced and by a conversation with peasants about mirages, although he stated 'I wrote *The Black Monk* without any despondent thoughts, out of cold deliberation. I just felt like describing megalomania.' The plot recounts the mysterious appearance of a spectral monk to the mediocre philosopher Kovrin, which has the effect of convincing him that he is somebody special. His wife and father-in-law contrive various remedies which have the result of banishing both the spectre and Kovrin's reason for living. He is only happy when he begins hallucinating once again, as a consequence of the tubercular complaint from which he eventually dies, but which, like his vision, is his greatest friend and solace – a compensation for his own mediocrity.

There is something of a reversion to Tolstoyanism in the theme of *My Life* (1896), Chekhov's longest fictional work since *The Duel*, and a work with strong political implications in so far as the hero, Poloznev, revolts against the whole pattern of vulgar provincial life in rejecting a position in the privileged class and opting to become an ordinary worker – a house painter. His marriage founders, he is disowned by his father and is left at the end disillusioned but unrepentant. The hero is a natural Christian: one of the meek whom, one suspects, Chekhov would like to inherit the earth.

This concern with the lives of simple people is continued in a series of narratives which have a peasant or low-life background. The best known are *Peasants* (1897) and *In the Hollow* (1900) although an earlier tale, *Murder* (1895), should also be seen in this company. This latter story concerns a tendency among Russian peasants to indulge in religious ecstasy as well as acts of violent amorality, as simultaneous aspects of intense religious devotion. A Christian fanatic, Yakov, shares with his cousin Matvei an hereditary inclination to religious ecstasy. Interrupted at his prayers, Yakov and his sister batter Matvei to death, watched by Yakov's idiot daughter. Yakov is sent as a convict to Sakhalin where he comes through suffering to recover his sense of faith.

The powerful, semi-documentary impact of *Peasants* (1897) can be gauged from some of the details of the deputy censor's report at the time: 'It paints too gloomy a picture of the peasants resident in our villages. They have no rest all summer . . . half-starved . . . drunkards to a man . . . cruel to their wives . . .

mutilate them ... oppressed by taxes ... blind to religion ...
totally illiterate ... worse off now than they were in the days of
serfdom'. Chekhov views a year in the life of these peasants
through the eyes of the heroine Olga, whose husband Nikolai, a
waiter at a Moscow hotel, is forced by illness to return to his
native village with his wife and daughter.

The miseries of the emancipation of 1861, comically referred
to by Firs in the second act of *The Cherry Orchard*, are here seen
to be veritable miseries indeed as the peasants are mortgaged to the
government 'unto the third generation' and bear a burden of debt
and collective responsibility which chains them more effectively
than any manacles of serfdom. It was a fact that the famines of
the 1890s were worse than at any time since the 1840s; peasants
tended to die younger, and alcoholism and venereal disease were
rife. The alienation felt by Olga and her family is intensified by
their smattering of education, and the sense of human dignity
they have acquired in the city, but despite the bestiality and the
harshness of this world, Chekhov manages to convey a sense of
the humanity of those condemned to suffer more than others.

In the Hollow, which was enthusiastically reviewed by Gorky
and much praised by Tolstoy, deals with the clash between an
emerging industrial society and rural peasant life. It focuses on a
typical rich peasant family of 'kulaks', the Tsybukins, whose near
relative builds a brick factory and exploits the peasants. A kind of
moral contamination spreads through the family, whose fate
forms the central theme of the narrative. The ugliness of peasant
life is, however, relieved by the presence of the gentle, oppressed
Lida, and a simple carpenter, as well as the sense of the redeeming
power of the natural world. As Donald Rayfield has suggested,
the story shows a Russia in which, in the final analysis, the
peasantry is the only real force, their destiny significantly different
from that of the intelligentsia who form the subject of Chekhov's
plays.

In 1898, Chekhov embarked on a unique project — the creation
of three separate stories which together make up a trilogy. Each
has a tale told by one of three narrators to one or both of the
others. The first, *The Man in a Shell*, is a story, according to
Chekhov's notebooks, of 'a man in a capsule, wearing galoshes, his
umbrella in a cover, his watch in a case, his knife in a holder.
Lying in his coffin, he seemed to smile — having attained his ideal.'
The story concerns a teacher of Ancient Greek, Belikov, a grotesque and at the same time sinister individual, whose tyrannical,
authoritarian spirit recalls that of Sergeant Prishibeyev. He is the
perfectly arrogant, servile reflection of the authoritarian order

which enslaves him. In spirit and in detail this is one of Chekhov's most Gogolian narratives.

The second story, *Gooseberries*, is a tale of the storyteller's own brother, a variant on Belikov, who slaves and half-starves himself in the city, buoyed up by the contemplation of a Gogolian idyll in the countryside, where he dreams of owning a small estate and growing gooseberries. He eventually achieves his lifetime's ambition, but the gooseberries turn out to be sour. In a reference to the moral of Tolstoy's fable *How Much Land Does a Man Need*, the narrator concludes: 'It is often said that a man needs only seven feet of ground: but really it's a corpse, not a man, that needs those seven feet. . . . a man needs not seven feet of ground, not an estate, but the whole world, the whole of nature.'

The final story, *Concerning Love,* looks forward to the theme of *Lady With Lapdog* (1899), and concerns the love of a lifetime which overtakes one Alekhin but which he allows to pass him by. He falls in love with the young wife of his friend, a court official: she reciprocates his feeling, but they do not declare their love for one another and indulge, instead, in bouts of agonized self-questioning and tormented moralizing. Finally, the official is posted to a distant province and only at the point of departure do the lovers dare to express their true feelings, by which time it is too late.

The subject of *The Bishop* (1902) had been in Chekhov's mind for the previous fifteen years and many of its elements hark back to stories such as *Easter Eve* and *Typhus* (1887). According to one of Chekhov's biographers, S.N. Shchukin, Chekhov described the story in the following fashion' 'A bishop holds morning service on Maundy Thursday. He's ill. There is a full congregation. The choir sings, the bishop reads the lesson on Christ's Passion. . . . He suddenly feels downhearted, feels he's soon going to die – may die this very moment. This feeling – whether through the sound of his voice . . . or through the other channels invisible and unintelligible – is communicated to those who are officiating with him, and then to the worshippers: first one, then another and finally to all. Sensing the approach of death the bishop himself weeps and his whole church weeps with him.'

Chekhov's final story of importance is, significantly, a positive one. The main emphasis is on Nadya who, responding to the influence of her friend Sasha (a figure very like Trofimov in *The Cherry Orchard*) begins to question the values of her provincial way of life. She abandons illusions about her mother and her fiancé and leaves for the university city of St. Petersburg, where she intends first to study and then to dedicate her life to society.

a: Primary Sources

Plays

Details of first Russian publication and of all English translations of individual plays are given under their titles in Section 1. The standard translation below is there cited under the short title *Oxford Chekhov.*

The Oxford Chekhov, Vols. I-III, translated and edited by Ronald Hingley (Oxford University Press, 1965-68). [Although critics quibble over the idiom of Hingley's translations, his editions of the plays have two distinct advantages over the rest of the competition in that every single one of the plays is included, and their unity as a group is apparent through the very fact that they share the idiom of a single translator. These are also far and away the best edited versions of the plays in existence although, regrettably, all the extremely valuable editorial material is only available in the hardback editions].

Short Stories

In addition to the full collection assembled in *The Oxford Chekhov, Vols. IV-IX*, translated and edited by Ronald Hingley (1965-80), there are four accessible and in-expensive volumes published by Penguin Books, under the title stories *Lady With Lapdog, The Kiss, The Duel,* and *The Party;* and two American Signet paperback editions, *Selected Stories* and *Ward No. 6 and Other Stories.* To these should be added two selections from the *Oxford Chekhov,* edited and translated by Ronald Hingley and issued in paperback form as *Chekhov: Seven Stories* and *Eleven Stories.* Among more recent editions of Chekhov translations are *Peasants and Other Stories*, ed. Edmund Wilson (New York, 1956); *The Unknown Chekhov*, trans. Avrahm Yarmolinsky (London, 1959); *St. Peter's Day and Other Tales*, trans. Frances H. Jones (Capricorn Books, 1959); *Early Stories*, trans. Nora Gottlieb (London, 1960); *The Image of Chekhov: Forty Stories*, trans. Robert Payne (New York, 1963); *Seven Short Novels by Chekhov*, trans. Barbara Makanowitzky (New York,

1963); *Late-Blooming Flowers and Other Stories,* trans. I.C. Chertok and Jean Gardner (New York. 1964); *Chuckle with Chekhov,* a selection of comic stories by Anton Chekhov chosen and translated by Harvey Pitcher in collaboration with James Forsyth (Swallow House Books, 1975); *Tchekhov: Plays and Stories,* trans. S.S. Koteliansky (London: Dent, 1967); and *Chekhov: the Early Stories, 1883-1888,* chosen and translated by Patrick Miles and Harvey Pitcher (London, 1983). All 13 volumes of Constance Garnett's translations of 147 of Chekhov's stories, first published between 1916 and 1926, are shortly to be reissued by Ecco Press.

Letters

The Life and Letters of Anton Tchekhov, trans. and ed. S.S. Koteliansky and Philip Tomlinson. London: Cassell, 1925; New York: Benjamin Blom, 1965. [As well as containing about 300 of Chekhov's letters, there is also a translation of 'Chekhov and the Theatre', written by his brother Michael.]

Anton Chekhov: Letters on the Short Story, the Drama and Other Literary Topics, selected and edited by Louis S. Friedland. New York: Dover, 1966. [This is a reprint of the 1924 edition and consequently does not take account of material which has become available in subsequent editions of Chekhov's work published in the Soviet Union. However, it is the only volume of its kind in English and its sectional divisions make it a most convenient reference book.]

Anton Chekhov's Life and Thought: Selected Letters and Commentary, trans. M.J. Heim, selected, introduced and with a commentary by Simon Karlinsky. New York: Harper and Row, 1973. [This includes some of the material which is available in Friedland's edition but is not so conveniently edited. However, it is better translated and has excellent explanatory commentaries.]

Letters of Anton Chekhov, selected and edited by Avrahm Yarmolinsky. New York: Viking, 1973. [This is probably the best selection of Chekhov's letters available in English although, like the Karlinsky and Heim edition and unlike Friedland's, it is not divided into sections, so is more difficult to find your way around, and the editorial work is nowhere near as exhaustive as the Heim and Karlinsky edition.]

b: Secondary Sources

Contemporary Theatrical Background

S.S. Koteliansky, ed., *Anton Tchekhov: Literary and Theatrical Reminiscences*. New York: Benjamin Blom, 1965. [Companion volume to *The Life and Letters of Anton Tchekhov*. The sections on the theatre consist mainly of memoirs written by directors and actors connected with the Moscow Art Theatre.]

Constantin Stanislavsky, *My Life In Art*, trans. J.J. Robbins. Harmondsworth: Penguin, 1967. [Chapters 34, 35, 37, 43, and 44 deal with the famous productions of Chekhov's four major plays at the Moscow Art Theatre between 1898 and 1904.]

Constantin Stanislavsky, 'Chekhov's Influence on the Art Theatre', 'Memories of Chekhov', 'Messages about *The Cherry Orchard*', in *Stanislavsky's Legacy*, ed. and trans. Elizabeth Reynolds Hapgood (London: Eyre Methuen, 1981).

The Seagull by Anton Chekhov: Production Score for the Moscow Art Theatre by K.S. Stanislavsky, edited with an introduction by Professor S.D. Balukhaty, translated from the Russian by David Magarshack. London: Dennis Dobson, 1952. (An indispensable volume for any serious student of Chekhov the dramatist. It contains an extended introduction covering the first production in 1896, the founding of the Moscow Art Theatre, and the famous revival in Dec. 1898. The bulk of the text is taken up by a translation of Stanislavsky's elaborate production score which can be read alongside a translation of the play on the opposite page. As well as the complete *mise-en-scène*, the text reproduces Stanislavsky's own ground plan and sketches for individual scenes.]

Edward Braun, *The Director and the Stage*. London: Methuen, 1982. [Chapter 5 is a useful synoptic account of Stanislavsky's work on productions of Chekhov's plays.]

V.I. Nemirovich-Danchenko, *My Life in the Russian Theatre*. London: Geoffrey Bles, 1968. [Part I, 'Anton Chekhov', and Part 2, 'Birth of the New Theatre', provide a vivid insight into Chekhov's relationship with the Moscow Art Theatre through this account by its co-founder, who was also responsible for introducing Chekhov's plays into the Art Theatre's repertoire.]

Marc Slonim, *Russian Theater: from the Empire to the Soviets*. London: Methuen, 1963. [Useful general history, in which Sections 2-3 (on nineteenth century background) and 4-5 (on Moscow Art Theatre) are especially relevant.]

General and Critical Studies

A. Heifetz, *Chekhov in English: a List of Works by and about Him*. New York, 1949.

David Magarshack, *Chekhov the Dramatist.* London: John Lehmann, 1952. [The first major treatment in English of Chekhov the playwright, it has stood the test of time and has been reissued by Methuen. It contains Magarshack's famous formulation of the contrast between the early and late plays as between those of 'direct' as opposed to 'indirect' action. Of all the full-scale studies of Chekhov's drama this is the only one to give decent consideration to the one-act plays, and still makes more interesting reading than the same author's later *The Real Chekhov* (London: Allen and Unwin, 1972).]

R. Yachnin, *The Chekhov Centennial: Chekhov in English, a Selective List of Works by and about Him.* New York, 1960.

Maurice Valency: *The Breaking String: the Plays of Anton Chekhov.* Oxford University Press, 1966. [This is the only study of Chekhov's plays which sets them amply in the context of nineteenth-century Russian drama as a whole and, as such, it performs a valuable service. It also makes useful connections between Chekhov's prose writing and his plays.]

Robert Brustein, *The Theatre of Revolt.* London: Methuen, 1965. [Contains a long essay on Chekhov, with particular detail on *Three Sisters* and *The Cherry Orchard*.]

Harold Clurman, *The Naked Image.* New York, 1967. [Contains an interesting account of his work on a production of *Uncle Vanya*.]

Robert Louis Jackson, ed., *Chekhov: a Collection of Critical Essays.* New Jersey: Prentice-Hall, 1967. [One of the best of the *Twentieth Century Views* series, containing, alongside academic exegeses from Soviet, British, French, Scandinavian and American sources, valuable essays on the plays in performance.]

Raymond Williams, *Drama in Performance.* London: Watts, 1968. [Revised and extended version of an important book, first published in 1954, by one of the first academics of distinction to stress the factor of performance in the study of drama. Chapter VI takes Stanislavsky's production score of *The Seagull* as a starting point for consideration of the important effects of the nineteenth century naturalist movement in determining certain kinds of approach to theatre production.]

J.L. Styan, *Chekhov in Performance: a Commentary on the Major Plays.* Cambridge University Press, 1971. [A moment-by-moment account of the later plays as imagined in performance conditions.]

Harvey Pitcher, *The Chekhov Play: a New Interpretation*. London: Chatto and Windus, 1973. [A stimulating approach to the major plays, which challenges the views of those who tend to stress the pessimistic side of Chekhov and overlook the humanist who is interested in portraying human relationships.]

Donald Rayfield, *Chekhov: the Evolution of His Art*. London, Elek, 1975. [One of the best and most coherent accounts of Chekhov's creative work viewed as a whole.]

Ronald Hingley, *A New Life of Chekhov*. Oxford University Press, 1976. [The most recent and, probably, the definitive biographical account in English of Chekhov's life and work.]

Beverly Hahn, *Chekhov: a Study of the Major Stories and Plays*. Cambridge University Press, 1977. [A sensitive exploration of key themes in Chekhov's less well-known fiction, as well as some of the better-known works, and in two plays, *The Cherry Orchard* and *Three Sisters*.]

Harvey Pitcher, *Chekhov's Leading Lady: a Portrait of the Actress Olga Knipper*. London: John Murray, 1979. [Part I and II of the book (up to 1905) consist of an absorbing account of Chekhov's developing relationship with Olga Knipper, who, as well as creating the roles of Arkadina, Masha (*Three Sisters*), Yelena, and Ranevskaya, also became Chekhov's wife.]

Jean-Pierre Barricelli, ed., *Chekhov's Great Plays: a Critical Anthology*. New York University Press, 1981.

J.L. Styan, 'Realism In Russia: Nemirovich-Danchenko, Stanislavsky, and the Moscow Art Theatre', and 'Chekhov's Contribution to Realism', in his *Modern Drama in Theory and Practice, Vol. I, Realism and Naturalism*. Cambridge University Press, 1981.

Victor Emeljanow, ed., *Chekhov: the Critical Heritage*. London: Routledge, 1981. [Fascinating selection of articles and reviews tracing Chekhov's reception in Britain and America from about 1910 until the end of the Second World War.]

Vera Gottlieb, *Chekhov and the Vaudeville*. Cambridge University Press, 1982.

Peter Holland, Laurence Senelick, and Leigh Woods, 'Forum: Symbolism in Chekhov', in James Redmond, ed., *Themes in Drama 4: Drama and Symbolism* (Cambridge University Press, 1983).

Richard Peace, *Chekhov: a Study of the Four Major Plays*. Yale University Press, 1983. [The most recent account of Chekhov's drama by a well-known scholar who has written extensively on nineteenth-century Russian literature.]